# Garfield Flats

## VERONICA HORTON

# Garfield Flats

Jeanie & Larry,

Enjoy!

Roxine

## CHAPTER ONE

# SPOONING

**"C**ome spoon with me," he beckoned from the bed. He looked sexy in his faded jeans and torn T-shirt, with his flaxen hair slightly disheveled over his steel blue eyes. He lay on his side with his head propped and resting in the palm of his left hand. His right hand reached out to me.

I stood by the window looking out as the foliage became intense colors of cobalt, magenta, and emerald. Nature had cast its black light effect just before the storm. Drops of rain started hitting the glass, first a sprinkle, then more blending into sheets of water flooding before my eyes. I turned and looked at him; it was impossible for me to say no. I moved away from the window toward him and as I took his hand, I slowly lowered myself next to his body; forming the spoon curve he had requested.

"Closer," he whispered in my ear. Gently lifting my hair and kissing the back of my neck, his strong hand pulled me in by my hip. I felt the curve of his body and smelled the fragrance of his skin. He moved his hand under my shirt, and as he touched my waist I felt my temperature rise.

"What're you doing?" I coyly asked, not wanting an answer.

"Oh nothing," he laughed mischievously and continued the abduction of my clothing. As he lifted my tie-dyed shirt over my head, his soft kisses progressed across my shoulders. My stomach fluttered as my body heat climbed to higher levels. Outside the wind started to pick up, making the rain slam against the window harder.

"The perfect music to make love by," he whispered in my ear.

"Oh James!" I moaned, "I'm a virgin… You know I'm not ready to do this right now."

"Baby, just relax. You'll have to give it up sooner or later. Might as well be sooner," he teased in the most alluring way.

"What if I get pregnant?"

My head was feeling heavy. I started drifting asleep with the distant sound of his voice. He whispered my name again, but I had become too tired to respond.

"Mia," he said gently, then a little louder. "Miiiiaaaa." The pouring rain continued and a crack of lightning shook the building.

"Mia! Wake Up!"

"James?" I opened my eyes. "What just happened? Was I talking in my sleep?"

"Yes! And no, you're not pregnant." Debbie's sarcasm never missed a beat. "If you keep having these dreams, you may need to get on some birth control!"

I ignored her. Those conversations never went anywhere.

CHAPTER TWO

# MOVING IN

My name is Mia Carlson, and my roommate is Debbie Benancasa. We met about a year ago working in the Unit Control Department at Young Quinlan's Department Store in downtown Minneapolis. It's a pretty posh surrounding for two struggling singles. Debbie stood at about five feet two inches, by wearing three-inch-high heels and teasing the top of her hair to sideshow proportions. Her Greek descent blessed her with rich, flawless beauty; along with that self-confidence I envied and longed for. Her body language demanded respect, letting everyone know that she was not one to tangle with. Her wit was unstoppable and she was damn loyal. Our friendship was tight. I'm five feet eight inches in my bare feet; our difference in height often drawing second glances. My hair was out-of-control curly, and my waist was a slight indentation melding into invisible hips and stick legs. My smile was my best feature, straight teeth and no braces. Debbie would often remind me, "Smile, do the best you can with what you've got." I worried that I would be mistaken for a stoner rather than self-confident. Debbie agreed the smile could be misleading, but suggested I stay with it. Debbie was "big city" mentoring me out of my "small town, farm girl" persona. We clicked.

We had just moved into our apartment building, Garfield Flats, in the Uptown area. It was located across the street from the bus stop with only a fifteen-minute bus ride to our jobs downtown, making it the perfect location.

Our place was small in comparison to the upper duplex I had just moved out of on Freemont Avenue. Garfield Flats was three stories high with four one bedroom flats on the first two floors and three flats and a laundry room on the Garden Level. Garden Level being the operative term for sub-basement. A brick and shingle exterior projected a more serious, professional nature than the tenants it held within. Sharing a one bedroom dwelling wasn't exactly what Debbie and I had in mind, but it was what we could afford. We rented flat 4G, conveniently located right next to the laundry room.

Our furnishings were sparse. We each brought our own twin-size mattress with no box spring or frame, but just enough comfort for a good night's sleep. There wasn't much room for any type of dresser so we had two laundry baskets at the foot of each mattress: one for clean clothes, the other for dirty. Debbie brought a black and white TV with a twelve-inch screen sitting on a rickety, portable metal stand with rollers. There was something loose in the wiring of the old TV, so Debbie's parents had given it to her in favor of a new one. On occasion, it would work if we gave a slight jiggle to the stand, sending a vibration to the wires within the TV. We really didn't watch much television though. By the time we got home from work there was only news, and that was usually depressing, all doom and gloom. After that were family shows, of which we had no interest. By ten thirty we were ready to put on our pajamas and tune in to the Tonight Show with Johnny Carson. This was a must, because the next day at the water cooler, Carson's monologue was always the topic of conversation. Debbie advised me that it was important to be "in the know" and any contribution to the conversation would make us appear experienced. It was a matter of social acceptance to watch and thus when the TV's condition became problematic, we needed to react quickly. Alternating nights, we managed to work around its mechanical challenges. One of us would lay on the floor in front of the TV and when we lost reception, gave the stand a nudge, kick or tap with a foot; bringing it back to life. Being in this horizontal position would account for many times of waking up at 3:00AM in front of the TV to the sound of hissing and a test screen in place of The Johnny Carson Show.

However, there were times when we didn't dare take any chances on the unpredictable mechanics of the television. For instance, the night Johnny had Burt Reynolds on as a guest, Debbie and I packed overnight bags and headed over to her parents' house for the night. Her mom made stuffed pork chops, green bean casserole, and whipped potatoes. For dessert, we had chocolate pudding with whipped cream. By the time Johnny Carson came on, Debbie's dad had gone to bed. He had to get up early in the morning and said he didn't have time to watch such silliness. Debbie's mom, on the other hand, stayed up with us. She put on her flannel pajamas, popped some popcorn, made root beer floats, and snuggled in with Debbie and me on the sofa. Not a word was spoken once Burt was on and the three of us sat in silence, swooning at his handsome looks and laughing at his every joke.

Debbie was a Neil Diamond fan all the way and hung a poster of the "Brother Loves Traveling Salvation Show" on the wall above her bed. She also kept a record player next to her bed and liked to play the album every night before going to sleep. "Sweet Caroline" was one of Debbie's favorite songs. She would sing that song in the shower, at the bus stop, on the bus, and just about every place in between. It got a little repetitive at times, but I got used to it.

A poster of James Dean hung over my bed. He was gorgeous; I loved him! I sang nothing.

On our list of needed purchases was: a sofa for the living room, coffee table and card table with chairs. Debbie said a sofa was a very strategic piece of furniture.

"It's virtually impossible to entertain without one!" she said. I knew very little about entertaining. I assumed she was referring to *her* love life, seeing as though I had none. Debbie's had a tendency to run hot and cold. We were optimistic, to say the least.

Living in a garden level flat allowed for little privacy, so we tacked up old sheets for curtains. Debbie's mom gave her a couple of old pots for cooking, but most of the time we lived on sandwiches, toast and cereal. She also gave us four forks, four spoons and four knives, saying that the more you have, the more you will dirty. She made sense. Our interests were far from building a nest, and the less time we spent in our humble abode the more we liked it. We were ready for adventure; we just needed a place to hang our hats. It wasn't much, but it was ours and we loved it!

CHAPTER THREE

# OUR DAY OFF

It was Saturday morning; the time we looked forward to since Monday; a day to kick back with nothing planned. I poured myself some coffee and sat on the floor, watching the raindrops hit the parking lot pavement.

While Debbie counted the money in her wallet, she asked, "As soon as the storm passes, ya wanna head to Uptown and grab some breakfast at the Embers?"

Uptown was the Minneapolis version of New York's City's Greenwich Village, anchored at the crossing of Lake Street and Hennepin Avenue in South Minneapolis. This made for the perfect location for a bus crossing, where numerous passengers could transfer from one to another and hop scotch across the Twin Cities for the price of a quarter. The intersection provided a perfect locality for eclectic groups of people, shops, and entertainment. Living in Uptown fulfilled my coming of age destiny. I had two favorite places to eat in Uptown. The first was Bridgeman's Ice Cream Parlor, my love for hot fudge sundaes started around the age of six. If there was nothing to do on a Sunday afternoon, there was always the option of ice cream. My other favorite was the Embers Restaurant on 26th and Hennepin. They had the best French fries and were open twenty-four hours a day! It was a great place for people-watching and the food was greasily to die for.

"Hmmm. Maybe. I'm thinking we should go down to the corner market and buy some donuts. Easier on the budget" I replied. Since I had moved away from home, I was forever paranoid of running out of money. Trying not to live beyond my means was a daily challenge.

"We can do that tomorrow. Time is of the essence. Never leave a stone unturned," Debbie said.

If there was one trait that Debbie hoped to have of mine, it would be the art of colloquialisms; she attempted to use them as often as possible, but sometimes fell short on the reference.

"Looks like it's starting to let up; let's blow this bicycle stand," she said.

"Popsicle stand," I said. Debbie grimaced at my correction. She still hadn't mastered the knack, but I tried my best to coach her.

I was fairly easy going and agreed. Before leaving, we needed to stop on the second floor and pick up our extra key from Bonita, the building caretaker. She was in her late twenties, about five feet five, tan, brown hair and eyes, child bearing hips, and the personality of a Bitch with a capital B. Her apartment was located directly above ours and the heavy thumps of footsteps made us more than aware of her presence. When we moved in, she told us her husband Tyrone was going to have a duplicate key made. "The last tenant only turned in one," she told us, as she stood in her doorway with body language telling us that we could go no further.

"Don't we need to worry about him coming back to use it?" I asked, apprehensively.

"Not unless he breaks out of prison," She barked, making it clear she didn't want to engage in any explanation.

"Ya'll moved in… ladies?" Bonita inquired with a fake Southern accent, adding to her questionable nature.

"Mmmhhmmm," Debbie answered in a mocking Southern whine. Bonita caught the sarcasm and reacted in a split second by slamming her door in our faces.

"Holy crap Debbie! We don't want to get on the wrong side of the land-lord our first week here!" I exclaimed.

"Don't get your buns in a knot," Debbie said. "She's only the caretaker. The hired help. Her façade of a Southern accent don't mean shit to me."

As usual, Debbie knew where she stood on the pecking order of life. As we stood, once again, knocking on Bonita's door; I started thinking about our encounter the day before. Knowing that I was living in a convict's old apartment gave me pause. What caliber of people had visited the apartment? Were they surly convicts from his past? Did they know their "friend" had moved to the Big House? Were there elicit dealings of an unlawful influence? Feeling queasy as the seconds went by, my stomach started making strange growling noises.

"What the heck is that?" Debbie whispered to me with a smirk tweaking the right side of her mouth.

"Never mind," I whispered, "some things can't be controlled."

"Does that happen often?" she asked, snickering.

"Drop it!" I scowled.

We could hear muffled noises from the other side of the door, then silence. The door suddenly opened. A young guy in his early twenties; with a bronze complexion; brown eyes, about five feet ten, with hair so black it shined, stood before us. His white T-shirt showed off his biceps, a tattoo of "Mom" on his right arm, and a pack of Camels tucked under his short sleeve rested on the other. A tiny diamond in his pierced ear caught a glint of light. I surmised he may have been the last of a dying breed of Greasers, but he was drop dead gorgeous regardless. Oddly we heard the sounds of

"Chicago" quietly playing on the stereo. The brass section bringing up the beat of "25 or 6 to 4" seemed a decade out of place for the hood in the doorway.

*"Da do ron ron ron, da do ron ron"*

"Hi," Debbie started, "We just moved into 4G." She shot me a glance and I began holding my breath for fear she would go too far with the small talk, forgetting our initial agenda.

"So, you must be Tyrone." She continued with sweetness in her voice that was more than predictable. An intensity of rage danced behind Tyrone's pupils, and his nostrils flared like a stallion. I sensed that he didn't want to engage in conversation of any kind. He grabbed the pack of Camels from his shirt, flipped the box open, and gave it a shake so the end of a cigarette emerged. Grabbing a filter with his teeth, he removed one from the half-smoked pack. We watched intently. His every muscle became involved in the action. He pulled out a book of matches that was tucked between the foil and its contents. With one quick strike, a spark, and spit erupted from the small torch and ignited the cigarette, which now hung between his lips. He took a drag while his eyes remained engaged with our presence. Leaning forward, he exhaled, filling our faces with smoke.

"Who wants to know?" He asked.

Debbie's charm was getting us nowhere, as we gagged on the blue haze. I, the forever peace maker, exhaled and informed him of our key situation. "Bonita said we should pick up our spare key today." I tried to get the words out as quickly as possible, attempting not to cough and hoping my stomach wouldn't send out another alarm. Without a word, he closed the door in our faces. Debbie and I stood motionless.

"What does that mean?" I asked.

We stood in the hallway, not sure of what we should do. We could hear muffled conversation on the other side of the door and decided to stand there a few moments longer.

The door opened again and Tyrone was nowhere in sight, now replaced by Bonita. She filled in the door frame like a linebacker. Her face was sullen; she gave us a cold stare. Quickly extending her fist like a prize fighter, she made us wince and duck in reflex. Unfortunately, our reaction caused us to lose our balance and stumble into the wall behind us. Bonita watched us with sheer delight, threw her head back, and cackled like a witch. Releasing the spare key from her grasp, it dropped to the carpeted hallway floor. We watched the jagged metal fall and bounce once. We stared, unable to move and pick it up in Bonita's presence. She then closed her door with a spooky kind of calmness, and that was that.

"Did we just enter the Twilight Zone?" I asked Debbie.

"Maybe," she replied.

CHAPTER FOUR

# THE EMBERS

**B**efore leaving for Uptown, we returned to our flat, making sure the extra key worked. The rain had stopped, but we knew it was just a matter of time before it would start again. I grabbed a baggy flannel shirt to go over my tie-dyed tee and tucked my crazy, wild hair under my Minnesota Twins ball cap, a gift for my 17th birthday; my dad loved baseball. I was good to go. Debbie, always the epitome of fashion, wore platform shoes, faded bellbottoms, and a stylish Mary Quant blouse with a crochet sweater. She grabbed her yellow paisley umbrella as we headed out the door.

A ride on bus #17 brought us up to Hennepin and 26th in less than 15 minutes. The Embers was packed, typical for a Saturday morning. Standing at the cash register was a gentleman wearing black pants, white shirt, and black tie. A manager nametag saying "Bill" was pinned just above his breast pocket, which held a plastic casing with two ink pens. He was greeting and directing patrons to various tables as they entered.

Giving us the once over he asked, "Are you here for the rally?" Already his eyes had moved beyond us and were surveying the people coming in behind us.

"Yep," Debbie replied before I could even process the question.

"What the heck are you doing?" I whispered in her ear.

She shushed me and whispered back, "Follow my lead."

The last time Debbie told me to follow her lead we snuck out the back of a restaurant, sticking a couple of guys with the bill. Debbie was a no nonsense kind of gal; but her sense of adventure sometimes scared the crap out of me.

Bill directed us to a group of about twenty people who were gathered in the back of the dining area, eating donuts and drinking coffee. We grabbed a couple of cups off a small cart, and I poured us each a coffee from the bronze carafe. Once we took our seats, a plate of donuts was passed our way. A man, presumed to be the head of the gathering, stood before the group. He dressed as though he had been on a long, laborious journey searching for fossils in the deserts of Egypt. Khaki pants, a button-down shirt and bomber jacket. His face had a five-o-clock shadow, covering a tan complexion; his eyes peered through wire-rimmed, rose tinted glasses. With his hand, he brushed his sandy blonde hair back off his forehead and addressed the group. His voice was calm and his demeanor was authoritative. "It's almost time to leave for Coffman Union. We have the banners and signs already loaded up. Now, remember, this is a Peace Rally. No violence. We want our voices heard and our veterans to come home."

The Vietnam War had appeared to be ending throughout 1969, but in early 1970, President Nixon authorized the invasion of Cambodia, bringing more American soldiers home in body bags and killing innocent Cambodian civilians. Many hated President Nixon, feeling his actions only exacerbated conflict. Campuses across the country were exploding with protests and rallies. Kent State in Ohio put every student across the nation in fear of their freedom after shootings from police had killed four students and wounded nine others.

Along with many college campuses across the United States, Coffman Union at the University of Minnesota was known for being the meeting place for war and civil rights protests, speeches, and rallies. Attending a peace rally induced fear right down to the core of my being. They had been known to turn into anarchy on occasion.

"We have to get out of here," I whispered to Debbie.

"It's cool. We've got nothing better going on. I've never been to one of these rallies; we can take the city bus back if we don't like it."

Her mind was made up and I knew nothing I could say would change it. After a donut and a half cup of coffee, we trailed after the group outside; following them as they dispersed to their various forms of transportation. We hopped into a Mini-Van with childlike flowers painted all over its rusted exterior. Crawling over worn out Persian rugs, which covered the metal floor of its gutted interior; we quickly found our spots. Two guys followed us into the van and sat to the right of Debbie. Each had hair past their shoulders and scruff on their faces. They sat cross legged and their boney knees stuck out through the rips in their jeans. They each had a guitar, and one of them had painted on the back of his, "Stop the Bombing." Propping them on their laps, they busily started fine tuning.

Next entering the van were three college aged girls, crawling quickly past us and huddling in the corner. All three are wearing faded corduroys and baggy, hooded sweatshirts. They looked like they were stuck in a high school state of mind; I surmised they had decided the attire for this event collectively. They whispered quietly amongst themselves, as if they were in a deep conversation of freedom.

The next person in our group appeared young, but was wearing the clothes of someone much older. His wing tipped shoes were scuffed and looked a size too big for his feet. His shirt had a button-down collar and his slacks were of a sales clerk style. He was clean shaven and his hair was short and nicely groomed. He sat calmly with his eyes closed; I feared he may have possibly had deep-seated issues with the propensity to become radical at any moment.

Once the van was in motion, the two-man-band started strumming their guitars. Their harmony worked well together, but after two blocks of the Buffalo Springfield song "For What It's Worth," I wished I had stayed home. I turned to look at Debbie and saw that she was locked in a stare at the wing-tip shoe guy.

"Debbie," I whispered, "stop staring. What are you looking at?"

"I always knew that guy was a fake," she whispered back.

"What are you talking about?"

"That pan handler with the long beard who hangs out at 6th and Market."

"Yea, what about him?"

"It's him. That guy over there." She hushed, "Only he doesn't have his fake beard and ragged clothes on… I knew he looked familiar."

"Are you serious? Crap, I gave him my lunch last week."

"What was it?"

"What was what?"

"Your lunch. What was in your lunch?"

"A peanut butter sandwich and some potato chips."

"I can't believe what you eat. How do you stay so skinny?"

"Debbie, what are we doing here? I feel like we're on our way to a funeral. This is the end. I just know it."

"Don't you have, like, a steady diet of peanut butter and honey toast?"

"Stop talking about my food!"

"Don't you get constipated from all that peanut butter?"

"No!" I answered, totally insulted by the implication.

"When was the last time you ate a vegetable?"

"1962…what difference does it make!?"

I began to freak out as quietly as possible, trying not to draw attention from the others. The rain was beating down hard on the metal roof of the van, a deafening prelude to a tragic fate.

"Would you chill?" she ordered me. "When we get to the rally, if we don't like it, we'll hop a bus back to Garfield. Simple."

Nothing was ever simple when Debbie was on a role.

After four versus of the Buffalo Springfield song, we arrived at our destination. The guitar players had stopped their singing, but the lyrics and melody remained playing in my mind.

At the University of Minnesota, a large crowd had gathered in the park in front of Northrop Auditorium, where a stage had been constructed out of plywood and two by fours. There wasn't any age: young couples, middle-aged adults, high school and college students, even some elderly, were all there. They appeared cold and wet, but determined. Their faces were serious with concern.

*"Somethings' happening here, what it is ain't exactly clear."*

Debbie and I huddled under her umbrella as the rain lightened to a steady drizzle. A girl, looking to be in her twenties, approached me with a smile.

"Hi, don't I know you?" She asked, looking at me somewhat mystified.

"I don't think so." I smiled back.

She was wearing a makeshift raincoat out of a black garbage bag with holes cut out for her head and arms. It hung mid-thigh, allowing her cut out for her head and arms gauze sack dress to appear from underneath, stopping just above dirty socks and sneakers. Her right shoulder secured a fishnet purse and her left hand held a sign that read "Make Love Not War." She mixed well with the surroundings.

"Sure!" she insisted, "We met last weekend. I was waiting outside the Nankin restaurant for the bus and you told me how much you liked Chinese food, too. I said I had just eaten the best moo-goo-gai-pan and you said your favorite was chicken chow-mein, then I said, Wow, what a coincidence because my mom likes chicken chow-mein, and you said you were going to call me. …Then…"

"Does the bus come soon?" Debbie mockingly interjected.

"I'm pretty sure you have the wrong person," I insisted.

Debbie started snickering and joined in. "I agree. You have the wrong person."

I always knew when Debbie was about to implode from containing her laughter. We had done it many times at work, like children in church. The harder we tried to behave, the harder it became to regain our composure. Debbie was having one of those moments. I wasn't

"Mia, take your hat off." Debbie ordered, just as she lost all self-control over her laughter.

"What? No, my hair will go crazy."

"Take the hat off!" Debbie repeated, bringing her hysteria to a small snicker.

"Fine." I obeyed defiantly taking off my ball cap. As I'd predicted, my hair was frizz, and kink, from roots to ends.

"Satisfied?" I asked, irritated at what I presumed to be the implication, and ignoring the childlike hippie chic in our company.

"Oh." The girl said, frozen in place. "I thought your voice sounded a little high-pitched. Sorry."

"That's it? That's the only thing that tipped you off?" I responded in disbelief.

Embarrassed, she turned and disappeared into the crowd.

"She thought I was a guy? I can't believe… she thought I was a guy!"

"Well, believe it," Debbie said, "and don't ever wear that getup again."

"Hey, Saturdays are my day off from being responsible." I defended my appearance while gathering and twisting my hair, tucking it back under my Twins cap. "I thought we were going out to breakfast, not protesting the war!"

Debbie knew I was agitated but, as usual, chose to ignore me. We both turned our attention to a man walking onto the stage. A peace sign was painted onto his army green rain cape that looked like it was made from rubber-coated canvas. It was hard to see his face with the hood pulled up. His pants were sewn out of an American flag, and looked offbeat with his Converse high tops.

The stage was equipped with three microphones across the front, perfect for a lead singer and two backups. Large speakers sat on each end, facing the crowd. He picked up a long, yellow extension cord that connected to a generator and plugged it into a larger black cord, connecting to the sound equipment. He fumbled a bit as he started adjusting one of the microphones, sending a piercing sound of feedback through the air.

"Testing, one, two. Testing, one, two." He repeated the words in a low voice, getting everyone's attention. Guys started whistling loudly, and women started cheering; I could feel the intensity in the air beginning to grow. After a few more adjustments, he began to speak: "Welcome!" his voice echoed. "Can everyone hear me?" The crowd cheered as though someone had just crossed a finish line. "We gather here today, not in violence, but as peace makers!" The crowd cheered again, pumping their signs up and down. I was literally shaking in my bones from the elements wet chill, and the activists' anger. I knew it was not the right place for me to be. I thought of my mom telling me, "Trust your gut." My gut was telling me to leave, yet there I stood.

"We must confront the President and force him to withdraw from Vietnam. This is not our war!" The voice that had been testing the microphones with a calming behavior had now turned a corner and was intensifying the moment. A chill was coming over me again, only not from the rain. I wanted to be anywhere but here.

*"What a field day for the heat. A thousand people in the street. Singing songs and carrying signs."*

The man continued, "Our voices must be heard and we must stand united for the brotherhood of man!" The crowd's cheers became deafening and the man continued, "And now, without further ado, please welcome…"

At that moment, a Molotov cocktail was thrown from the crowd, landing on stage and exploding in front of one of the microphones, sending a resounding BOOM through the amplifiers. It was followed by another homemade bomb that echoed its Doppler Effect all over campus and beyond. Causing instant pandemonium everyone took off running in different directions. Not knowing which direction to go, or where we were going, Debbie and I were separated in the chaos.

*"Stop children, what's that sound? Everybody look what's going down."*

I ran until I was out of breath, making it to 14th Avenue and 4th Street. I was dead center in the campus village of Dinkytown. Tiny shops filled the area for anyone who needed anything while living a campus lifestyle. Restaurants, bars, and apartment buildings housed the University students, making up for a large part of the quaint area. The name Dinky was used literally. Grays Campus Drugstore was dinky, but had most of what was needed. The Dinky Dome was a small theological seminary. The Sound of Music was a small store holding every album recorded within the past ten years, as well as something to play it on. The Dinky Theatre had four rows of seats. It had been rumored that Bob Dylan lived somewhere in the small city, but I didn't know where. Before this moment, I would have loved hanging out in Dinkytown and fantasizing about running into him. Now, my fantasy was to return to my flat.

Ducking into a city bus shelter enclosed with Plexiglas, I was hoping I didn't have to wait long before I could catch a bus back to Garfield. I took a seat on a wet bench and started counting the change from my pocket. I figured it would take a quarter to get back home; I had a dollar twenty-five in change. The rain started in again and I was chilled to the bone, waiting impatiently for a bus. Any bus.

A police car slowly rolled up, stopping right in front of my fleeting shelter. For a brief moment, I imagined an irate bus driver pulling up behind him, giving him the horn. I watched the officer as he tried to dodge the rain drops, entering my space. Looking up at him, he seemed to be about five feet eleven, clean shaven with glasses. His build was heavy with a truck driver's belly. A donut ring of hair appeared just below the rim of his hat. He didn't look old enough to be my dad, but more like an uncle. His voice was bland and nondescript. I was worried.

"Where you headed?" he asked.

"South Minneapolis, sir."

"Are you a student here?"

"No sir."

"What are you doing here?" His tone began to change.

"I came for the rally, sir."

"Without an umbrella or raincoat?"

"Well, I wasn't planning on coming here, I…"

"What exactly *were* you planning?"

He gave me a look of disapproval and I wasn't sure where things were going.

"It all started when I was having donuts and coffee."

"Are you being smart with me?"

"No sir, no smart intended."

"You better come with me."

"What?"

"You heard me, now get in the car before I cuff you."

There are two things my parents drilled into me before I moved away from home.

**1.** Don't take rides from strangers.

**2.** Don't argue with the law.

I had done a slam dunk without even trying. The officer stood behind me and pushed down on my head as I climbed into the back of the squad car. I couldn't tell if I was shivering because my clothes were dripping wet or because I was a nervous wreck. I was clueless as to what was going on. I sat obediently, afraid to move, while the officer wrote on his clip board. The storm was picking up momentum and the rain was pelting down on the roof of the squad car. I was reminded of the hippy van I had been in only an hour ago, but it felt like it had been days. Heat was blasting from the dashboard and started drying the water off of my face, making me feel welcomed in a satirical way. Like I was waiting in the rain for an Archangel to rescue me, but the devil pulls up instead, and hell feels so warm and inviting.

> *"Paranoia strikes deep. Into your life it will creep. It starts when you're always afraid. Step out of line the man come and take you away."*

The policeman finished writing on his clip board and gave a sigh, as though he had just eaten a turkey dinner and was ready to sit in front of the box for a televised football game. Static started crackling over the CB radio, breaking into a woman's voice:

Dispatch: "Charlie 22, how do you receive? 10-2."

Officer: "This is Charlie 22 go ahead."

Dispatch: "We have a 10-55 (drunk driver) who is possibly 10-96 (mentally ill) and is wanted for a 10-97 (theft) officer needs 10-32 (backup) 10-16 (reply)."

Officer: "This is Charlie 22, 10-4 (affirmative) I'm on my way."

Charlie 22 flipped a switch and the dual cherries on the hood of the squad car started spinning their red flash. His lead foot hit the gas pedal, and with sirens blaring, we flew down University Avenue with the power of a 426 Hemi engine.

Taking the corner at high speed, we fishtailed down Lyndale Avenue. The centrifugal motion catapulted me involuntarily across the back seat of the car, slamming me into the side. "Ow!" I cried, but Charlie 22 was ignorant to my plight. He screeched to a halt, which slammed me forward against the back of the front seat. I bounced back with my ass landing right where I had started. "Man," I commented to deaf ears.

Parked halfway on the side walk was an old beater of a car with no back window. I recalled my dad telling me "It's the little things that get you every time." The arresting squad car was stopped alongside of it. The culprit stood against a brick building with his palms on the wall and feet spread apart. A twenty something man with long, wet hair tucked behind his ears and a soaked T-shirt that revealed his boney structure, proved he'd been standing in the rain too long. Faded jeans barely held on to his slender hips and knobby toes peeked out from the straps of his earth sandals. A young police officer, looking wet behind the ears literally, stood behind him with his gun drawn. Charlie 22 walked over as I sat silently, locked into the back seat of the squad car. Charlie 22's approach looked commanding, and the few words he said to his colleague, I was unable to hear. He then slapped a set of cuffs on the offender, grabbed him by the scruff of his neck, and threw him into the back of the other squad car. The two officers then engaged in a short conversation and Charlie 22 then returned. As he slipped into the car I felt a slight lean in the chassis. Making a note on his clip board, he mumbled to himself "Rookies." The radio static began again and an agitated dispatcher started talking:

Dispatcher: "Charlie 22 How do you receive, 10-2?"

Officer: "10-4 go ahead."

Dispatcher: "We have a 10-86 (domestic upset) at Paudeen's Wings, location at Lake and Hennepin."

Officer: "Did you say a 10-86 at Paudeen's Wings?"

Dispatcher: "10-4."

Officer: "The chicken place?"

Dispatcher: "10-4 (affirmative). Apparently, a husband and wife got in a dispute over the extra crispy and the wife's large derriere. She got so upset she pushed her husband and he fell to the floor. Paudeen herself called in the complaint."

Officer: "Is the husband ok? 10-2."

Dispatcher: "Paudeen said once the husband was down the wife sat on him. She's refuses to get up, 10-2."

Officer: "Can he breathe? 10-2."

Dispatcher: "Paudeen said the wife is sitting on his buttocks. He's complaining that his legs are going numb. 10-2."

Officer: "10-4 I'm on my way."

When we arrived at Paudeen's Wings, I once again remained locked in the squad car while my escort went inside. The aroma of fried chicken engulfed the building like a heavy fog, sending my stomach into a tailspin. So far, I had only had a donut and half cup of coffee and we were long past lunch. The thought of a greasy chicken wing made my mouth water.

Charlie 22 finally walked out of Pauleen's Wings with Minnie the whale and Flat Stanley in tow. I panicked at the thought of sharing the back seat with an angry couple and reminded myself to take long, deep breaths. To my relief, the couple walked over to a navy blue, Chevy Nova, got in, and started the engine. Without wasting any time, the 10-86 slowly puttered out of the parking lot without their bucket of chicken and not so much as a wave goodbye.

Charlie 22 returned to the driver's seat, missing another downpour by mere seconds. Once again, he began etching on his clip board like an artist. Grabbing the radio receiver, he reported in:

Officer: "Dispatch this is Charlie 22; how do you receive 10-2?"

Dispatch: "10-4 go ahead."

Officer: "10-86 has been resolved. I have the 10-19 in custody and returning to Precinct One. Do you read 10-2?"

Dispatch: "10-4."

Charlie 22 hung up the receiver and I finally had the guts to talk.

"Excuse me sir, what is a 10-19?" I asked nervously.

"Bombing suspect," he replied without expression.

"I'm a bombing suspect?!" Goosebumps began to rise on my arms and legs. Beads of sweat were forming above my lip and on my forehead. A twitch, and my left index finger was tapping out of control. What will I do now? How will I spend my days in jail? Will I ever meet the man of my dreams? My thoughts were running wild. I feared I was losing all control of my life, my future. Charlie 22 gave me no response.

*"It's time we stop, hey, what's the sound?...Everybody look what's going down."*

## CHAPTER FIVE

# PRECINCT ONE

**M**y choice was to either stand or sit on a bench bolted to the floor. Too nervous to sit, I stood. Leaning against the cold cell bars, I thought that it would be a good time to have a harmonica. My only knowledge of jail cells had been watching The Andy Griffith Show. This place wasn't even close to the warm, fuzzy feeling conveyed on TV!

I was sharing a cement and iron space with a collection of less-than-desirable men. Once again, my gender had been mistaken, but for safety's sake I kept it that way. The clock on the wall read 6:30. Odd that anyone would need to know the time in here.

The jingle of keys and the clickitty-clack of footsteps gave me a glimmer of hope that I would be released. A young man, who looked to be in his early twenties, appeared in front of the cell. He had a ring of keys and started to fumble with them, trying to find the right one. A seedy-looking cellmate snickered at the officer's naiveté and couldn't stop himself from harassing the kid.

"Hey, punk, aren't you supposed to be home in bed?" The surly, poor excuse of a man couldn't stop himself from harassing. After all, he was already behind bars.

The officer was nervous and fumbled the keys even more. "Hey," the cellmate continued, "aren't you gonna miss 'Leave it to Beaver?' You better get on home." The officer's blood pressure was rising and a shade of bright red was covering his face. He accidently dropped the ring of keys, which evoked a roar of laughter from the derelict. Although agitated, the officer picked them up and succeeded opening the door on the third try. He then looked over the collection of gruff subjects behind bars, moving slowly to each one. When he looked at me, our eyes linked a lengthy stare. I guess he sensed that I wasn't where I should be. I froze, waiting to see what was to happen next.

The redness began to fade and a flesh color returned to the officer's cheeks. Pointing with authority he chose me and five others to follow him down the hall to another room. He handed each of us a number as we entered another room, where a window like mirror covered a large portion of one wall. Without instruction, we fell into formation, as though we all watched the same episodes of "Dragnet." Three bright lights hung from the ceiling, giving little reflection of a grey, spackled backdrop. With our numbers in hand, we mechanically held them in front us. I looked at the others in the line-up and realized we had very similar tastes in fashion. Jointly we wore various styles of faded jeans, T-shirts covering our plaid flannel shirts, and a ball cap to top off our ensemble. Again, the officer gave me a peculiar glance. He paused, and then asked me, "Who was the officer that brought you in?" "Charlie 22" I answered. He made no other comment, ordered all of us to face the mirror, then left the room.

There I was, wondering if my last supper would be on a tin tray with canned peas and instant potatoes, or perhaps I would wear a stunning orange jumpsuit with a set of shackles from Harry Winston. I couldn't believe I was in this mess. Where was Debbie, anyway?! Was she in jail too? Shouldn't I get one phone call? I started to lose it. I started running numbers through my head as to who I should call. Who did I dare call? Who would be home to answer? I had no idea if Debbie was back at the flat, so

I didn't want to waste my one chance on her. Calling my parents was out of the question; they would freak before I could explain. My anxiety was building as we stood in awkward solidarity, for what seemed to be an eternity. Finally, a man's voice over the intercom began instructing us: turn to the right, turn to the left, then face forward. A momentary silence and the man spoke again "Number three, please step forward."

Oh my god, it was me! I was number three! What had I done to deserve this? I looked at my card, double checking the number, then walked closer to the mirror, as requested. My knees were shaking so badly; I could barely stand. "Would you remove your cap, please?" The voice asked in a polite manner. I took off my ball cap and my hair fell to my shoulders, immediately expanding to Janis Joplin proportions.

"Number three, you're free to go."

"What?" I responded in disbelief.

"Please walk over to the door." The mystery voice instructed.

The door opened and Charlie 22 was standing in the hall, looking at me with a disapproving stare. I obediently walked over to him and sheepishly said, "Hi."

"I think we should have a talk. Follow me." he ordered. I obeyed like a lost pup, following him down the hall to an elevator. We took it to the second floor and I followed him without further instruction. We walked past heavy, mahogany wood doors with frosted glass inserts. Each one had a name etched in black ink, stereotypically men with a title.

At the end of the hall we entered into a large room. The temperature was tropical and the hiss of the radiators played like calming music. Double hung windows were opened just enough to let in the cool fall air. Several desks resembled what I would have envisioned as a man's secretarial pool to be like. Each desk had a chair made of oak with worn leather seats, anchored by brass upholstery tacks. The arms were worn and had lost their luster of finished wood. Swiveling on four heavy spokes supported by castors, Charlie's chair squeaked when he sat down. He had me take a seat on a hard, grey metal chair, next to his desk full of clutter. I glanced at the empty paper coffee cups and crumpled papers that filled a tin wastebasket. A candy wrapper of a peanut butter cup caught my eye and I was reminded of how hungry I was. Then thought of Debbie's comment about my peanut butter diet. Then, thinking of the whole day… I was mad. I tried to change my train of thought and focus on a bulletin board hanging in front of the room, just like the one I had in grade school. No papers with foil stars stuck to them on this bulletin board though, only black and white pictures of wanted criminals.

"It appears I've made a mistake" Charlie 22 grumbled. "The **man** we are looking for is described as wearing something similar to your getup. This could have been avoided, had you told me you were a female."

I wanted to state my case. I wanted to tell him: "In the first place, I had no idea why you arrested me! AND, where the hell are my Miranda Rights?" But I would have to be Debbie to pull that one off, and of course I thought of what my dad said, "Don't argue with the law." I had a gut feeling that if I opened my mouth at this stage of the game, it would only make things worse. I decided to cut my losses and take the lecture. Quietly, in my mind, I recapped the events of my day, starting with Tyrone blowing smoke in my face and ending with being mistaken, for the second time, as the opposite gender wearing a 'getup'.

My life was going down the toilet.

## CHAPTER SIX

# RETURNING TO 4G

As it turned out, I didn't need to make a phone call. Charlie 22 told me he would be driving me home, once he was done with his paperwork. My stomach started growling, but I didn't know if it was nerves, or if I was just plain hungry. I slumped down in the steel chair, trying to get a little more comfortable, but feared I looked too apathetic I would set myself up for another lecture. Charlie 22 looked up from his desk and reached over to open the desk drawer between us. "Pick one," he said.

I looked down to a variety of snacks. There were Mounds bars, Almond Joys, Salted Nut Rolls, Mallo Cups, and miniature bags of Mr. Peanut peanuts. His generosity to share his stash of sugar overload could have been thought of as an act of kindness, or maybe just pity. Whatever it was didn't matter and I didn't hesitate for fear he might change his mind. I chose a Pearson's Nut Goody. He suggested I get a paper cone of water from the cooler next to the window.

I took my last sip and Charlie 22 asked, "You 'bout ready to go home?"

I'd been ready to go home since I'd left that morning.

"Yes, sir," I answered.

I followed him out, of what I assume, was the back door of the building. Like a lost animal weary from wandering, I stood behind him as he unlocked the squad car door, expecting to be put in the back seat. Instead he gave me a glance and with his hand, and motioned for me to go to the other side and hop in the front. Just as we pulled out of the lot, a number 17 bus passed us.

"That's my bus!" I burst with excitement.

"You don't need to take the bus tonight. Not safe to be standing out front of the police station at this hour."

Who would have thought crime would happen in front of a police station? I was wet, cold, and in no condition to argue.

Riding in the front seat of the squad car proved to be far more comfortable than the back had been. Charlie 22 seemed genuinely concerned for my well-being and even offered to swing by the Red Barn Restaurant for a sandwich to go. I declined. I was looking forward to being back in my own space, anticipating peanut butter and honey toast; taking a hot shower, and climbing into my bed. When we arrived in front of my building Garfield Flats had now taken on a new semblance. This morning it was just a place I rented. In just one day it had transformed to my safe place. Charlie 22 looked at me and offered a piece of advice: "You're in the city kid, keep your eyes wide open."

I obediently nodded and got out. He waited until I was safely inside; I turned and waved; he gave me a nod as he pulled away. I stood for a moment in the entry, watching the tail lights of the squad car go down the block, then I turned and headed downstairs to my flat. I slipped the key in the door and recognized it wasn't locked. I had hoped Debbie was home, and just forgot to lock it, and that I wasn't going to be greeted by a convict who had just broken out of prison.

I heard unfamiliar voices, as I closed the door behind me. To my regret, several strangers were sitting with my roommate, cross-legged, in a circle, on the floor of our living room. There were two guys and two girls I didn't know, and Debbie. I stood in silence, wondering who "they" were and why "they" were with Debbie in the flat. When Debbie finally noticed me, she squealed with animated delight.

"Mia! Holy cow, where have you been?!"

Approaching me with arms extended, she gave me an unexpected hug. "I've been worried sick!" she exclaimed for all to see.

"I can tell." I snapped back, sarcastically. I wasn't in the mood for company. I wasn't in the mood for explaining. I just was not in the mood.

"Hey, really, is everything ok?" she said looking me dead in the eye.

"It will be. I'll tell you all about it tomorrow." I gave her a long stare and then shifted my eyes toward the group. She ignored my indication of concern and continued with her perky, happy self.

"Sure, I dig that. Listen, I want to introduce you to some very cool people. We met when I stopped for a breather after running my ass off from the explosion. I'm thinking it was karma that brought us together. There they were, catching their breath, same as me! When I looked back, I expected to see you behind me. My god, it was scary!" Debbie was very keen on karma and believed she had a sixth sense about everything. I had always thought her sixth sense was more conjecture, but I didn't see any point in stating my case.

"Oh, cool." I tried to smile with my response. *I wanted them to disappear.*

Debbie started her introductions with the guy who was sitting closest to her. "This is Revolution," she said. His auburn hair was pulled back in a ponytail; a horseshoe mustache framed his upper lip; and bushy eyebrows hovered over eyes that peered through horizontal slits, shaded by heavy lids. His smile was affable, yet I sensed an undertone of deceit. His clothes were sloppy and in need of a washing. He gave me a nod, and without uttering a word, lifted his right hand to the air, extending a peace sign.

"Next to Revolution is Cosmic River," Debbie continued. Cosmic River's skin was sheer porcelain with freckles sprinkled across her cheeks. Her straight, blonde hair dropped almost to her waist and she looked dwarfed in size sitting beside Revolution. Her lips were full with a pigment that matched her rose-tinted eyeglasses. She smiled at me sweetly, and jutting her hand into the air, gave me a peace sign in silence.

"Over here we have Hyacinth," Debbie pointed, as though I was unable able to follow the direction of the circle. Hyacinth resembled a bud, more than a flower. She wore layers of clothing but didn't succeed with the hopes of camouflaging her plump figure. Her hair was twisted up, and secured with a piece of leather and a stick. Her cherubic face and shy smile relayed a note of innocence. Her violet eyes reminded me of the flowers in my grandma's garden, and the name Hyacinth fit her nicely. She held her arm into the air with the familiar peace sign, accompanied with silence.

Debbie then extended her hand with her palm turned up, as though a prayer should follow. "This is Ambrosia," she said. "He's visiting from California. His dad's a Hare Krishna."

"No kidding?" I said in mocking curiosity.

Ambrosia looked as pathetic as I felt. His skin was pale and his eyes were milky grey. He wore a sheet, wrapped around his bone thin body and his sandals were straight out of the bible's Pedi fashion line. He looked like he needed a good dose of sunshine, and possibly a carrot. I had thought I'd seen the last of these people on my trip to California last summer. It never occurred to me that they would actually migrate to Minnesota. Unlike the three mutes before him, he stood up and gave me a hug saying, "Peace be with you, child." I surmised his Catholic roots had a tendency to leak out through his Krishna persona.

"And," Debbie continued, "drum roll please," she laughed, "there's me, Saffron!" Her arms flew up in the air, like she'd just landed off the balance beam. "Don't you love it!?" Her excitement was tiring and I was still clueless as to what they were all doing in our flat.

"Um, maybe." I answered, unable to stop my face from scrunching.

"Revolution thought of it. He says it's a spice from the Crocus plant that originates from Greece. Isn't that amazing?! I told him I was Greek and he immediately knew what flower I should be!"

Revolution sat, gloating on his intellect. I wasn't buying it. Debbie's exuberance struck my last nerve.

"Yep, he's a real botanist." I snarled.

She ignored my comment and continued, "We should think of a new name for you."

"I'm good, really...Crocus."

"It's Saffron."

"Oh, right…sorry… um, Mia works for me." I forced a half smile and looked at the group, without making eye contact, and said, "Nice to meet you all." Then excused myself as I headed for the bedroom.

Meeting Debbie's new found friends moved me to the point of total exhaustion. Not only was I NOT in the mood to eat anymore, but beyond too tired to shower. I slipped into my flannels and crawled into bed, pulled my blankets over me, curling into a fetal position. I glanced at my poster of James Dean and threw him a kiss. With a sigh of relief to be back in my own space, I reached over and turned out the light. I was spent.

CHAPTER SEVEN

# THE PLATOON

There were six women in the Unit Control department of the Young Quinlan Department Store. Celia Winningham was our boss. She stood at about 5'5," with most of her weight lying between her waist and knees. She failed her attempt to hang on to a more youthful appearance by dyeing her hair jet black, and wearing dark red lipstick upon a heavily-powdered face. The look was offset by large, ornate earrings, bangle bracelets, and gaudy necklaces. These were mostly gifts from her adult children, channeled through grandchildren, making it impossible for her to discard. Although she preferred to be called Celia, in hopes to fit in as one of the girls, her management position made it difficult to do so. Her desk sat at the end of a long corridor with three desks to her left and two to her right. Debbie's desk was directly to Celia's left, even though Celia referred to Debbie as her "right hand gal."

Next to Debbie's desk sat Mrs. Odettes. She was a sweet lady with severe osteoporosis, making her look closer to 80 years old, as opposed to the 60 she really was. She hated the stigma of being a spinster, and started using "Mrs." at the age of 40. As time moved on, the fact that she had never married became inconsequential and most of Young Quinlan's employees knew her story. She dressed impeccably and her taste in jewelry made Celia's look like she had once worked with the carnival. Every Thursday

Mrs. Odettes skipped her lunch break, allowing her extra time on Friday to go to the Paris Beauty Salon for her weekly shampoo set. When she returned, she was undoubtedly the happiest woman on our floor. An involuntary little hop occurred in about every fourth step that she took. This let us know how pleased she was with her new doo. We all loved Mrs. Odettes.

The desk next to Mrs. Odettes' was Alice Garcia. Her straight, golden blonde hair was bobbed just below her chin, and she had a face like Peter Pan. Her Scandinavian roots didn't stop her from marrying her handsome husband of Mexican descent. They had a baby not long ago, and she gave up smoking a pack a day; replacing her vice with bubble gum, chewing like it's going out of style. Her slight figure had started to take on more curves, and her desire to work had taken a back seat to motherhood. To the platoon's disappointment, she announced that she would be leaving come summer to become a full-time mom.

My desk was across the aisle from Alice, and next to me was Patty Chadwick. She used to be Patty Prentis, but she married her "prince charming" (as she kept reminding us) and, for strangers she requested, or more so insisted, to be called Mrs. Chadwick. She constantly obsessed over her makeup, fixing her hair, and touching up her lipstick. She kept a tiny mirror in her desk drawer, and snuck a peek every chance she got. Before she got married, all she could talk about was the upcoming wedding. After we had lived through that, she's bored us to tears with unending dissertations of how difficult it was to find the right house. She, and her husband, were ready to buy the American dream, before starting the American family. She was a text book Betty Crocker and Emily Post rolled into one. I tried to avoid her company during lunch, and coffee breaks when possible. Sometimes it worked out, but there were moments when I drew a blank on excuses and had been faced with eating my peanut butter sandwich to endless chatter of Colonial, Tudor, American Craftsman, and Queen Anne architecture. I grew up in a Ranch style home, with a tuck under garage. My parents raised me, and my siblings with a "be thankful you have a roof over your head and food on the table" sensibility. Searching for a particular style of house to raise children seemed redundant to me.

We were all very different in our personalities, which probably accounted for how we got along as a dysfunctional family. Some days we liked each other, some days not, but we would always come to one another's defense when needed.

## CHAPTER EIGHT

# BOUTIQUE SHOPPING

I ndian summer was a time that most Minnesotans dreamt of all year long. Fall had arrived, and all of the leaves on the trees had turned to crimson and gold. The nights were a crisp cool, just enough to wear something heavier than a sweater. The days were sunny and warm, like swaddled babies, often reaching perfect temperatures in the 70's.

As soon as I got off work, I decided to take a walk in the city, and meander my way over to the Unique Alternative Boutique. I headed over to LaSalle Avenue, enjoying the beautiful fall benediction along the way. I used to wonder what other people were off to do, after a day at work. Did they have families? Did they have other jobs? Were they as tired as me? But that day I didn't care. I was immersed in the magnificence of life.

As I passed every tree that stood in their small patch of earth, surrounded by cement, I marveled at their brilliance. The air was clean, and the cars that passed me on the street were silent. Their exhaust was nonexistent. A couple was seated on a bench, speaking in sign language. Their conversation flowed like doves in flight. I was briefly fascinated by their joy, but then I was once again captivated by the fall colors of the trees. As I rounded the corner at Ninth and LaSalle Avenue, I had looked back at the couple I'd passed only moments ago. They appeared to be miles away now, almost a lifetime.

LaSalle Avenue was a flash of history, mixed with current eras. An old bank building, constructed of stone like bricks, stood like a grandfather to the newer construction it was bordered by. Six marble steps invited you to enter through its double doors that boasted large etched glass inserts that read "A Unique Alternative." I was about to enter the store, yet I had no memory of having taken the stairs. I chose the door on the right, and as I pulled to open it I caught the reflection in the glass of a sports car pulling up to the curb. I hesitated momentarily, feeling I knew the man behind the wheel. I continued inside.

I paused as my eyes adjusted to the dim lighting, and rested, feeling as though I had been on a long journey. A large Tiffany chandelier hung in the center of the room, with matching sconces strategically mounted on the surrounding walls. A round tufted sofa sat in the middle, offering refuge to weary shopping partners. Racks of clothing were grouped from casual to formal wear, and placed in various areas throughout the boutique. The old hardwood floors creaked, but were soon silenced once I made it to the lavish Oriental rug.

I was immediately greeted by a very thin, tall, and serious salesgirl. She was dressed in a black sheath, with a black leather belt restraining her insignificant waist. Black boots completed her ensemble. Her black hair was straight, absent of movement, hanging to the middle of her back. Her complexion paled beneath black eyeliner, black mascara, and lavender lipstick. Had I envisioned Timothy Leary and Angela Davis having a child together, it would have been her. I flinched when she spoke.

"Welcome to *THE* Unique Alternative," she proclaimed. She had a ventriloquist's manner; her voice carried without a smile or change in expression. I was briefly impressed at her lack of muscle movement. "May I be of assistance in helping you find the perfect garment to embellish your cute, yet ever so impassive body?" she asked. I was astonished by her ability to offend and offer help in just one sentence.

I had been putting aside a little bit of cash for the past nine months, determined to have something spectacular for this year's holiday party. Something...remarkable. The Unique Alternative Boutique had a reputation for the uncommon fashion design. I ignored her insult.

"Something red," I requested.

"Predictable," she mumbled.

She pulled three different dress styles from a rack of formals; one was short and strapless in apple red; one was knee-length, and cap sleeved in cherry; and one was floor length, long sleeved, with a very low neck in cerise. I clutched the strapless and ducked into the dressing room, pulling its curtain closed behind me. Quickly removing my work dress, I slipped into the formal. I was pleased to see its built-in bra gave my figure more of a curve. The length stopped just above my knee and I was concerned about how short it could go if I sat. The satin was trussed up on my left hip, and secured with a large bow. It zipped up the back and I was awkwardly struggling with it when the sales girl threw her voice into my space.

"Do you need my assistance?" she questioned robotically.

"Maybe." I answered as I stepped out from behind the curtain.

"Let me help you." A man said as he got up from the tufted sofa and walked toward me. He almost smiled, but held back the emotion. His intense blue eyes saw my past, my present, and my future without a spoken word. His blonde hair was flawlessly combed in a roguish style. He motioned for me to turn around. I obeyed. I felt his touch as his hand brushed against my skin, grasping the top of the zipper. I moved my hands to my waist, securing the dress, and tilted my head forward. He gently eased the metal, securing its closure, and paused. Feeling his breath on the back of my neck gave my body a rush. His smoky scent mixed well with his powerful cologne. He whispered so the salesgirl was unable to hear.

"Where would you like to go?"

"I'm really not prepared to go anywhere," I whispered back.

"It looks to me like you're dressed for a party."

I tried to turn around to face him, but his right hand rested on my shoulder, holding me gently in place, as his lips made a connection with the nape of my neck. His left hand was now at my waist, pulling me in closer to him. My body became warm, as his lips moved their way across my skin. I felt as though I could have fainted, but managed to speak, "It would be nice to go for a drive, I guess."

"Then your chariot awaits, my lady."

He took me by the hand, and with only a thought, I was his passenger, sitting low in the 550 Spyder. The car was fast, and moved with ease on its way out of the city. The air was warm, and felt seductive against my bare shoulders. My legs were exposed, as the satin slipped its way from cover. I didn't care. I wanted him to see me. I wanted him to want me. He shifted the car and we reached a higher speed. His eyes looked straight ahead in full concentration, but his hand moved from the shift, resting on my leg, just above my knee. My breath was becoming short, and I wanted more. I wanted him to caress me. I wanted him to take me like no other man had. An intensity flared within me, and my desires were out of my control. His hand moved closer to my wish. I closed my eyes to the colors of fall splashing their brilliance. I could barely hold back what was happening. We arrived at a deserted road just outside the city, and he pulled the Spyder into a clearing. Without hesitation, he killed the motor. Turning towards me, he pulled me to him.

"I can't believe this is happening. I can't believe this is happening!" I blurted out half awake. I slammed my hand on the alarm clock that cried its wake-up call. 6:30 A M, time to get up and ready for work, but all I wanted to do is dream.

## CHAPTER NINE

# BUSINESS AS USUAL

**D**ebbie and I had been in our new place for a couple of months. We bought an old olive-green sofa, dated circa nineteen forties, from the Salvation Army for only fifteen bucks. We got two wooden orange crates from the corner store for a dollar, and pushed them together to serve as our coffee table, or rather, foot stools. Revolution owned a pickup truck and helped us get the sofa moved to our flat, which for some odd reason made him think he had roommate privileges. I was relieved when Debbie straightened him out in short order. The apartment was still sparse for furnishings; however, we were slowly piecing things together, being careful not to over extend our domiciliary spending.

Living next to the laundry room proved to be very convenient, but on occasion, problematic for us. Tenants doing wash invariably knocked on our door, asking if we had quarters in exchange for green backs. At first, we didn't mind, and would accommodate, but word spread fast. Soon, we had people knocking at all hours of the night, so Debbie came up with a business idea. We would give out change with an added finance charge, three quarters for each dollar. We made an "Open" and "Closed" sign and hung it on a thumb tack, just below the peephole, on the outside of our door. At first tenants started complaining, until they realized it was a take it or leave it situation. Our biggest problem was the midnight washers who lived down the hall, in flats 2 and 3G. They were zombie-like characters who had no regard of the time of day, and paid no attention to our sign. It was still up for debate if they could read.

One evening, there was a knock on our door when it was obvious we were closed for business. I peered out the peep hole and immediately recognized the disheveled zombie from 2 G. After the third knock, I figured I might as well deal with him, or his incessant behavior would continue through the night.

I opened the door to a barely cognizant, sad excuse of a human being. He was dressed in jeans and a tie-dyed tee-shirt. He smiled at me with his last meal stuck in the crevices of his crooked teeth. His eyes were murky brown, trying their best to focus, and his greasy hair was tucked under a ball cap with a peace sign hand-painted on the bill. He was disgusting.

"We're closed," I said. Looking at his hat, I became a little curious. It didn't seem to fit his persona.

"Interesting hat," I added.

"Yeah, I'm diggin it. Found it in the lost and found box in the laundry room." His breath was pungent and his voice was conducive to infected adenoids.

"You mean it wasn't yours, but you decided to just take it?"

"It was there for a long time, man. I figured I might as well make use of it. It was lost and I found it." He snickered as though what he had just said was hilarious. I failed to see the humor.

"Humph." I grunted. We both stood for a moment in silence, pondering. "Are we done here?" I continued. His presence was giving me the heebie geebies.

"Yeah," he said with a stoner's daze, "I'z wundrun if youz could give me sum change?"

"The sign says closed for business. That means… we have no change."

"You sure? Cause you might have some if you check."

"Check what, the abacus? We…have…no…. We're not a bank, ya know."

Unbelievably, he told me he was going to the manager to complain. Losing my patience, I shook my head and closed the door. The next day, Bonita's aggressive ignorance compelled her to pay us a visit. Her intrusive pounding could have been heard a block away.

I looked out the peep hole, "Yep, it's Bonita," I said to Debbie.

Debbie immediately jumped up from the couch and approached the door. "Step aside; I'll take care of this," she said. Bonita's arm was cocked and ready for another round of pounding when Debbie opened the door, ducking to miss a direct hit. I snickered at the close call, but Debbie's sense of humor was on hold.

Bonita began her rant, starting with, "Some of the tenants have been complaining. They think your finance charge is a little steep. They don't like your hours, and they have said you are both very rude to your customers."

Debbie held her hand up, stopping Bonita the same way she stopped traffic when she volunteered as a crossing guard in grade school. "Zip it Bonita." Debbie ordered. "In the first place, Mia and I are doing this because there's no change machine in the building, and there's a steady stream of losers knocking at our door. Seems the lazy ass caretakers won't give out change. In the second place, they aren't customers! They're wandering imps in the night! And last, but not least, YOU are the caretaker; the hired help; the clean the halls lady! You dig?! Don't think you can boss me around."

Bonita was stymied, and had no comeback. She didn't say another word, just turned, stormed down the hall, and stomped up the stairs back to her apartment. After slamming our door, Debbie turned to me and said in all seriousness, "Swear to me that you won't tell Revolution about this."

"Holy Crap!" I cheered "That was so far out! Did you see the look on her face? Wild! And the way you held your hand up. Wow, power! I love it. Take control of the situation! Debbie, that was sooo cool! I have to tell everybody. Wait. Why? Why not tell him?"

"Listen Mia, I'm serious. It wasn't very peaceful-like, and I know Revolution will get pissed."

"What's the big deal? Wait, isn't that an oxymoron? Him getting pissed at *you* for not being peaceful."

"I don't care what kind of moron it is, just don't tell him."

"Fine, if you insist, I'll take it to the grave."

I was miffed at Debbie's concern, and uneasy with the thought of any-one, much less Revolution, trying to control a person's personality. All in all, things seemed to be going smoothly, but it bothered me that she was becoming more involved with Revolution and the "flower children." I knew she was the old Debbie deep down inside, but this new relationship was putting a damper on everything we used to think was fun.

The group was visiting our flat more and more, making it very uncom-fortable for me to be home. My only escape was to spend time in the bed-room, shutting out their existence. Their influence had turned our flat into a Zen Den. Embellishments of macramé plant hangers held odd shaped bowls, made by Cosmic River. They hung in every corner of our apart-ment, making it look similar to a nursery discount store. She had yet to master the art of clay and wheel, but insisted we accept her gifts of rejects and deformity.

Colors of indigo blue, poppy red, and sunshine yellow, were splashed across two sheets, which were once white, and hung for curtains, obstructing our view of the parking lot. Evidence of their creation left marks in our porcelain tub, as though there had been a brutal murder. Sitar music played on our stereo from the moment the group arrived, until their departure. Revolution hung multi-colored beads from the ceiling, dividing our living and miniature dining spaces. Debbie sneered at me when I commented that the only thing missing was a crystal ball. Her sense of humor waned when it came to Revolution, and his followers, especially if they were in the room.

I envisioned, for myself, an imaginary warning track keeping me from crossing into the nucleus of hippiedom. I tried my best to respect Debbie's choice of friends, but preferred to keep some detachment. The four of them traveled as a pack, carrying a tapestry bag filled with odds and ends. When arriving at our flat, they resumed their roles, as though it was the only way they knew how to communicate. Cosmic River pulled a ball of twine out of her bag, and Hyacinth got out the tape measure. Talking in low voices, they discussed the strategy of yet another macramé project.

Revolution and Debbie huddled on the couch, blending as one, sharing a cup of herbal tea that smelled great, but tasted like dirt mixed with orange rind. They engaged in heavy conversations on peace, love, and the rights of the people. Without a hint or warning, Revolution would punch the air yelling, "Power to the People!" Cosmic River, Hyacinth, and Debbie duplicated the move.

Ambrosia claimed to be a non-conformist. He found his own space, and sat in a Lotus position with his palms turned up, resting on each knee. On the floor in front of him was a cone-shaped, cast iron bowl with a perforated lid. Incense would smolder inside, escaping through tiny holes, and swallowing up every cubic foot of fresh air in the flat. He started his mantra, while the smell of burning patchouli permeated my senses, confusing my headache of annoyance with lack of oxygen. I had reached a point where I could no longer take another breath, and I vocalized my frustration.

"It can't be good for our lungs to inhale that crap." I snipped at Ambrosia, taking out my frustration of the entire group on this poor, single, malnourished individual. Breaking his trance, he looked at me in defense. He then quickly retorted, as though he had been rehearsing his response for days:

"It says in the book of Revelations: another angel came in holding a censer of gold. He took his place at the altar of incense and was given large amounts of incense to deposit on the altar of gold, in front of the throne, together with the prayers of all God's holy ones. From the angel's hand, the smoke of the incense went up before God and with it the prayers of God's people."

I stared blankly at his bald head, and the sheet draped over his blue jeans and high-top sneakers. The Minnesota weather was moving into colder days and wasn't suitable for the Krishna fashion. Knowing he had my full attention, Ambrosia proceeded to stand up from the floor, raised his arms to the heavens and continued his dissertation, "Let my prayer come like incense before you, the lifting up of my hands like the evening sacrifice." Then he winked at me and said, "Psalm 141."

"Far out." I responded, unable to hold back my sarcasm. "Get to confession or you'll go to hell," I smirked, "Mom 1967."

With a confused look, he sat back down on the floor, elevated his feet to the crux of each knee, hands resumed their upturned position, and with a deep breath, continued to hum.

As a whole, the group was cool, I guess. I figured it could be worse, I could deal with it. Although they tried to pull me into their circle, I declined for fear I would lose what little personality I had finally acquired in my first year of independence.

## CHAPTER TEN

# ABSENT ROOMMATE

**W**inter was coming and the winds of change were arriving in more ways than one. Although Debbie and I saw each other every day at work, Revolution was taking up more and more of her time. Sometimes, she stayed at the flat, and other times she would spend the night at Revolution's "domain" as he jokingly called it. I had never been there, nor did I want to be, but I referred to it as "The Crypt" (when Revolution wasn't around). It was no secret to Debbie that I wasn't fond of her new-found love.

"You're just jealous," she'd say to me when I was in a mood. I would make no argument. In many ways, I guess I was. After all, she was my best friend, and now Revolution was taking up all of my time with her. I wanted to be happy that she had romance in her life, but I feared the romance was more control and manipulation on Revolution's part. And then it happened. She had been with Revolution all day on Sunday, and called me around eight that night.

"Mia, hi."

"Hi"

"So, I just wanted to call and let you know that I'm spending the night with Revolution. I'll see you at work tomorrow though."

"Oh, okay, what about your work clothes? Do you need me to bring them to work?"

"No…but thanks. I'm all set for tomorrow."

"Ok, well... See you tomorrow"

"Mia?"

"Yeah?"

There was a pause, and the hesitation made me worry. I knew she wanted to say more, but couldn't.

"I'll see you tomorrow," she said, and then the line went dead.

## CHAPTER ELEVEN

# NIGHT CAPERS

I was bummed, and really didn't feel like doing much, nothing new there. I had the apartment to myself most of the time, so I did pretty much whatever I wanted. There were no exchanges on whose TV show to watch; I watched whatever I wanted. What would I have for dinner? Whatever I wanted. I had started reading to fill the time, and I took my lonely self to the library once a week. The irony of sitting in a library where you can't really talk to anyone had me thinking way too much on where I was going with my life. I had checked out "Valley of the Dolls" because since I am now on my own, I'm allowed to read smut anytime I want. That, in itself, was the most audacious thing I had done on my own. Poor pitiful me.

After I hung up the phone from talking to Debbie, I slipped into my flannel pajamas and turned on my radio. Pulling back the tie-died curtains, I secured them with the macramé sashes that hung from hooks bored into the sheetrock. (I knew the moment Revolution came up with this decorative enhancement idea, it would be coming out of our security deposit.) Feeling melancholy I curled up on the sofa, and looked out at the parking lot. The shadows started fading into night, and appeared tranquil in a city sort of way. I started wondering, as I always did, as to where my life was headed. Having a relationship sounded like a fun idea. Someone to hold, or be held by, was a fantasy of most girls my age. My mother always told me

"Wait for Mr. Right, he'll show up." And of course, she would always throw in, "They won't buy the cow if they get the milk for free." I had no idea what attributes Mr. Right would, or should, have had. Nor was I interested in the cattle business, but I got the proverbial colloquialism and kept my patience, along with my virginity. Thoughts of my mom's advice came with comfort and a smile.

I drifted off to sleep, until the noise of arguing from the parking lot woke me up. It was pitch black outside now, with only the glow of a street light on the corner. I hadn't yet turned any lights on in the flat, so nobody would be aware that I was watching. Tyrone and Bonita were standing behind a pickup truck, unloading a large galvanized tub, sufficient enough to service water for at least a cow or two. Bonita had lost her grip, and Tyrone's shin caught the brunt of her fumble, sending him into a tirade.

"Can't you do anything right?" he belittled her with a brash, louder-than-whisper, voice.

"I guess not! I'm with you, aren't I?!" She roared her defense so that there was no mistake she was angry. Her seething rage could be heard throughout the parking lot and beyond.

"My mother was right," he mumbled.

"You really don't want to bring her into this, do you?!" Bonita was fit to be tied, and Tyrone was close to doing the tying. "That dishonest wench..."

Tyrone held up his right hand with his index finger pointing at Bonita, stopping only inches from her face, "Stop" (he jutted his finger)..."Right" (he jutted his finger again)..."There" he jutted his finger a little too far this time, touching Bonita's nose. With the reflex of a rattle snake, Bonita grabbed his finger and bent it backwards, bringing Tyrone to his knees.

"Apologize" she demanded. "Say...you're...sorry!"

Tyrone was like a child and began begging for Bonita's forgiveness. She released his finger from her grip, and Tyrone rose from the parking lot floor. Cement gravel crumbs stuck to the knees of his dirty jeans, but he didn't bother to brush them off. A truce led them both to silence. They proceeded to carry the watering hole to the back entrance. Their focus remained on getting the awkward shape through the door. Tyrone was limping with every step, cussing and swearing as the two moved with caution. I didn't think they would have noticed me, even if the lights had been on. I could hear them thumping up the back stairs, cussing and swearing at each other along the way. They had resumed their roles of codependent idiots. Tyrone was back to giving orders and Bonita was agreeable, but argumentative as usual. When they entered their apartment, there was a boom, and then silence. The tank landed on their floor, just above where I was sitting, and a crack took form in the plaster ceiling above me.

## CHAPTER TWELVE

# THE WINTER CARNIVAL

R umor had it that it was once said that St. Paul, the capitol of Minnesota, was as cold as Siberia. The politicians of the time decided, in order to ward of the "nay-Sayers", they would need to come up with an idea to make people want to visit their fair city. Hence, the St. Paul Winter Carnival began the winter of 1886. To this day Minnesotan's still freeze their ass's off for two weeks in January, proving to the nation how much fun it can be to live in subzero temperatures

CHAPTER THIRTEEN

# MRS. ODETTES

**M**rs. Odettes took her heritage very seriously. Her father was Irish, and to honor his memory, she joined the "Sisters of the Leprechauns." Every Saturday night at six o'clock she met with the Sister's at Kelsey's Bar for a bowl of Irish stew, and a mug of beer. They don't discuss anything in particular; it was just a comfortable connection. But, on March 17th, in the city of St. Paul, everyone was Irish. Celebrations typically started in the morning with a "St. Patrick's Day Parade." The Sisters of the Leprechaun's met in the early hours at Kelsey's, and would cook up huge pots of corned beef and cabbage. Knowing the importance of this day, Mrs. Winningham always gave Mrs. Odettes the day off from work, so that she could participate.

Once all the food was prepared, and ready to serve, the sisters would don costumes of green satin knickers, puffy white shirts, and vests that were made from Kelly green velveteen, and adorned with gold sequins. Top hats with glitter completed their leprechaun attire. Some of the sisters would work behind the bar pouring pitchers of green beer. Others would help serve up piping hot dishes of corned beef and cabbage to the large crowd, that would undoubtedly attend. Mrs. Odettes played the upright piano, and wore a crisp, tailor-made jacket over her vest, which gave her a Liberace feel. Her roster of Irish tunes was lengthy, but the inebriated crowd would request "Oh Danny Boy" at about every third song. Mrs. Odettes soprano voice would pull the crowd through the verses that weren't well known to the general public. She sang them with the emotion of a true Irishman.

Being an honest and loyal daughter, she felt it was her obligation to give equal time to both of her bloodlines. Her mother was full blooded Norwegian, and so Mrs. Odettes also joined the Daughters of Norway, a more passive group in comparison to the Sisters of the Leprechaun's.

On Saturday mornings the Daughters would meet in the church kitchen, and make batches of lefse that would be sold every Sunday morning at the Emanuel Lutheran Church bake sale. A list of the Daughters was always posted on the refrigerator in the kitchen, as to who is next on the rotation for bringing a casserole to be shared on Sunday night. They gathered at five o'clock, and after dinner, and general conversation, the daughters reviewed the morning's sales of lefse and other topics of business, such as the upcoming Winter Carnival Float contest.

## CHAPTER FOURTEEN

# MONDAY MONDAY

**Y**ou could have heard a pin drop as she entered the room. Debbie Benancasa had transformed into Saffron from head to toe. Her hair was no longer teased in a stylish pouf with a "That Girl" flip, but worn straight, parted down the middle, reducing her height to barely five feet tall. A head band of wooden beads, weaved between three leather shoe-laces, covered part of her forehead, and tied with a knot at the back of her head. Her Capezio shoes were swapped out for clunky, black boots that screamed Li'l Abner. Her cotton sack dress was brown with little yellow flowers, and hung to her ankles. She wore not a stitch of make-up, and her eyes looked bare and defeated. Her movement was determined, but her gate was out of sync. She was the unhappiest flower child I had ever seen, far from the spice of a Crocus plant than I had imagined. I was afraid to ask what happened to her designer coat, as she hung up an army green, double breasted maxi, which I assumed was from the WWII trunk show. It was a sad, sorry sight and everyone in the office was left speechless. Debbie gave me a look of "I dare you." I picked up on the vibe and kept my peace.

Finally, Mrs. Odettes broke the silence. She had been waiting for the whole department to be present before sharing her exciting news. Now was as good of time as any. Mrs. Odettes stood as straight as she possibly could, and with a deep breath she began:

"At last night's meeting of the Daughters of Norway, we discussed the upcoming Winter Carnival. As you know, every year we enter the contest for best liked float in the Torchlight Parade. This year's prize is $500.00. Emanuel Lutheran needs a new boiler, and although we haven't won in the past, we're going to give it another try. This year I've been appointed as chairperson of the decorating committee."

Celia declared, "How wonderful," and began clapping. "Girls, isn't that wonderful," she cued us. We all followed her lead.

Mrs. Odettes continued unexpectedly, "I know this is asking a lot, but the Daughters of Norway needs some extra help decorating the float. We would greatly appreciate any time any of you could give."

An uncomfortable silence fell over the room. At first Celia looked speechless. I'm thinking she was surprised that Mrs. Odettes took the authority of asking for help without running it by her first. But, holding true to her power, she took the liberty of speaking for us all. "We would be honored to help, wouldn't we girls?" Celia declared.

We were all speechless for the second time that morning.

## CHAPTER FIFTEEN

# REAL-ESTATE: NOT FOR THE FAINT AT HEART

He used a fake name on his calling card; something that would blend in the white man's world. His boss agreed it would be less problematic if he went with Joe or Jim Smith. He decided on Bobby Jones, thinking it had a nice ring to it. The ink was barely dry on his calling card when he got his first client, a young couple looking to purchase their first home. Piece of cake, Bobby thought. He'll have his first commission check in no time.

After meeting with the Chadwick's, Bobby had lined up four houses that met Mr. Chadwick's financial approval, and Mrs. Chadwick's esthetic necessities. He kept a pocket sized spiral pad, to make notes of their reactions, likes and dislikes, in his shirt breast pocket.

House one: Mr. Chadwick liked it. Mrs. Chadwick thought the kitchen was too small, and the stove was too old. The water pressure was good, but it took over a minute before the hot water reached the kitchen faucet. The old tin cabinetry would definitely have to be replaced, but would suffice for the time being. The refrigerator was in good working condition, but the freezer was too small. The lighting in the spare bedroom was dim, and would require sheer curtains with a shade for privacy in the evening. The bathroom had a nice size tub, but the free-standing sink had no counter space and could pose a problem. Medicine cabinet was too small and not deep enough. The master bedroom had limited closet space, and after measuring with the tape measure Mrs. Chadwick carried in her purse, there was only two feet around the perimeter of the bed from the wall. When Patty gets pregnant, and is in her eighth month, it could be an uncomfortable width. The attic added additional storage, but the stairs were scary. The basement was too damp. The back yard was nice, and fenced in, enough room for a swing-set with a slide, but the garden area lacked good soil. She knew this after she took a shovel out of the garage and insisted her husband dig a hole at least a foot deep. "We can't grow good vegetables in sand," she declared. There was only a ten-foot driveway that ran from the garage to the alley and Mrs. Chadwick's concern was not having enough vision of oncoming traffic. "It's an alley," Mr. Chadwick said in frustration, brushing off the dirt he acquired in the garden. Mrs. Chadwick started to sniffle, and avowed he didn't care about her well-being.

After spending three hours at the first house, the current owners returned, and Bobby and the Chadwick's had no choice but to leave. Their schedule for the next showing had been missed, and Mrs. Chadwick had become hysterical over her husband's lack of understanding. She insisted on canceling for the rest of the day, claiming to have had a headache.

This scenario continued for thirteen more houses, over the course of two months. Bobby Jones was second guessing his new profession.

## CHAPTER SIXTEEN

# NO WAY OUT

**D**oing my job should have been a fairly simple task. I kept the inventory books for women's designer wear, jewelry, men's shirts and belts. A bit of a mundane task, however, but low pressure was just the way I liked it. Sitting next to Patty Chadwick was the most difficult part of my job. She had been getting on my last nerve with her constant chatter about house hunting, and she had me on the brink of insanity. I wish I could have counted on Debbie for comic relief, but her new appearance had compressed her sense of humor. Sitting next to Patty for eight hours a day was affecting my conscious mind. I buried myself in my work to such an extreme that Mrs. Winningham had given me a ten-cent raise. My work hours were spent flying under the radar, and then it happened, I was caught off guard:

"What are you doing this Saturday?" Patty asked me in a sweet, but oh so irritating way. Normally this was a safe question to answer. Patty was married and had her husband for all recreational events in her life. Debbie and I had been able to be lax with our defense mechanisms, until now.

"Nothing special," I answered, "maybe get some groceries. I'm running low on peanut butter."

"How about you Debbie?" Patty asked.

"Nothing," Debbie answered, "do wash, hang out. Revolutions busy."

Then it hit me. This was a set up! Debbie and I spun our chairs around simultaneously, and looked at each other with the same realization, proving our telepathic connection wasn't completely lost. Debbie's eyes were the size of saucers, and my jaw had dropped uncontrollably. Like Siamese twins, we knew exactly what was going to come next out of Patty Chadwick's mouth.

"eeeeee!" Patty squealed and clapped her hands together. She then continued with her pitch.

"I thought we could go house hunting together. We should meet for breakfast, and then we can ride in my car. The first house is located at thirty sixth and Bloomington Avenue, and I'm to meet my realtor there at eleven Saturday morning."

"Oh gee, what a great idea." Debbie said, with her sarcasm starting to take shape. "Are you sure you want to go in your car? Wouldn't it be more exciting to take the bus, like us commoners? Oh wait, don't you have a husband? I mean, like, doesn't he want to help pick out where you might want to live…together…raising your children?"

Patty laughed, "Oh Debbie, you're so funny! Of course, Danny wants to see the house before we buy it. He just doesn't understand that there is a lot to consider, besides financing and structure. Like for instance the lighting. Sure, the house might look good at nine in the morning, but what is it going to look like at six o'clock at night. These things are important."

"It's the same house, turn on a light." Debbie scowled, shaking her head in disbelief.

"How many have you looked at so far?" I asked.

"Only fourteen." Patty answered, "It's a very tedious process." She pulled her compact out of her desk drawer and reapplied another coat of lipstick. At this point, she had the attention of the whole Unit Control department.

"Hmmmm, I can only imagine…tedious." Debbie commented.

"So, what are you girls going to wear?"

Patty doesn't wait for our answer, nor does she miss a beat assuming we'll be delighted to accompany her. My hippy roommate had now forgotten any vow of love and peace, and is ready to go for the jugular.

"Clothes work for me. How about you Mia? Clothes sound good to you?"

"Clothes work," I said, and turned back to my job at hand.

## CHAPTER SEVENTEEN

# THE EGG & I

It started off to be a typical Saturday morning; slept in till nine, then Debbie and I reluctantly got ready to meet up with Patty. I wore my favorite faded jeans, and a washed out navy pullover, with a tartan plaid scarf for warmth and a little panache. The weather was perfect for my fringed suede boots; I felt my self-confidence taking hold since I retired my "getup" of flannel shirts, and ball caps. I kept my opinions to myself when Debbie donned her latest sack skirt, and long crochet sweater over a long-sleeved top. She gave up wearing a bra prompted by Revolution's suggestion to be free. Today she had attained the look of a crocus in need of watering, but as I said, I kept my opinions to myself.

We met up with Patty at the Egg & I Café on Lyndale Avenue as planned. The door of the café sat in the middle of two large picture windows, and we could see Patty waiting patiently looking into a small compact, fixing her lipstick, and wearing an outfit that left us both dumbstruck.

As we entered, the gathering of hungry strangers was inviting, and the room was warm and smelled of fried bacon. In the center of the room were several square tables covered with black and white checkered oil cloth; each was surrounded by four yellow cane-back chairs. We were lucky Patty arrived ahead of us to save a place during a very busy Saturday morning rush.

On one side of the café, lined against the wall, were six small booths large enough for only two diners in each. Ten by twelve-inch cartoon sketches of egg type people, doing silly things, were framed, and hung on the wall above each one. On the other side of the café was a long counter with a row of chrome and vinyl seated stools, all occupied with heavy smokers. The cabinets, adjacent to counter against the wall, held several coffee pots, and shelves of coffee cups; a small refrigerator kept containers of milk and cream. Two juice dispensers offered orange and apple juices. Extra napkin holders, menus, and salt and pepper shakers occupied space next to juice glasses, waiting on a tray. The entrance to the kitchen was at the back of the room, with two retro style swinging doors with round windows, telling me the café had been here for a very long time. I'm reminded of an old movie with Fred Astaire and Ginger Rogers; I smiled at the thought of them dancing their way through at any moment.

Debbie and I pulled up a cane-back, and were greeted by an all too perky Patty. "Hi!" she said, with an exuberance we were unable to share. We started examining the menu without so much as a "Good Morning."

Patty immediately started in: "Well, do you notice anything different?"

"Nope, never been here before," Debbie answered.

"No, I mean about the way I'm dressed," Patty said. I remained staring at the menu, and held back my laughter; however, Debbie felt this was no laughing matter.

"I noticed," Debbie says, "what's your point?"

"Well," Patty began, what I feared to be, her critique on fashion, "I thought I would give you a better visual of the style you seem to be struggling to attain."

At this point, I was relieved Debbie didn't carry any sharp objects, or a concealed weapon.

"Oh please, do tell." Debbie sneered, with a glare in her eyes resembling that of a cat. Patty's ignorance was never failing, and she continued ignorantly:

"Well, for instance, I'm wearing a Bill Blass Moroccan Poncho; it's his latest in the Monterey Couture line. It's very warm, so I'm able to get away with wearing this light weight Hungarian peasant blouse. Feel the fabric, it's absolutely delicious." Patty holds her arm toward Debbie's direction; I flinch and yell, "OH GOD!" when Debbie reached to touch it.

"What the heck is your problem?" Debbie grumbled and shot me a look.

"Nothing," I said with a snicker, "I just thought…"

"I know what you thought." Debbie began grinning a devilish smile.

Patty continued without a clue: "I went with the wide-wale corduroy, gaucho pants, for added warmth; look how the chocolate brown shade goes so nicely with my brown leather knee-high boots, they're Halston. Can you believe I got everything at Young Quinlan's! Glenda on fourth floor said that all the high fashion designers are "taking a page", so to speak, from the younger generation. I even got the leather choker there. Isn't that amazing! Plus, you can use your employee discount! So see, you really can dress in style without shopping at that dreadful Gauze Conceptions. I assume that's where you've been."

*Gauze Conceptions was located in an old 1920's two story, Queen Anne style house, with a haunting appearance of chipped, and worn shingles, in need of repair. The four steps leading up to the front porch were weathered, and refused to let go of its old, yellowed lead paint. The shop within was owned by a young women, named Angel. She carried a line of apparel to fit the needs of any woman that was a square peg, trying to survive in a round hole world. Let's say you needed something for a stroll through an art festival; a simple number to make a statement, and looked upon as a peace loving.*

*Angel knew exactly how to transform you from working girl by day to trippy hippy by night.*

Debbie was insulted, and her glare intensified as her chin lowered. She peered above invisible glasses, and leaned forward ever so slightly, and said, "Gee, how illuminating...you are the essence of fashion...but...your choker seems a little loose; how about I tighten it for you?"

Patty reached up to her throat, and with a look of puzzlement and concern replied (with a somewhat squeaky voice): "It feels ok."

"Tell us about today's plan," I interjected quickly, trying to redirect the conversation.

Patty cleared her throat; changed her focus, and began chattering about the upcoming house hunt. "If we finish our breakfast early, I thought we could drive around the neighborhood of the first house, and see what it's like."

"No skin off my teeth." Debbie remarked, looking over the menu.

"Nose," I corrected, regretting my words, as soon as they spilled out of my mouth.

"Knows what?" Patty enquired with a dizzy naiveté.

"Nose... no skin off my nose," I replied. Patty was still confused, and Debbie rolled her eyes at me.

The waitress approached our table wearing jeans and a yellow, long sleeved tee-shirt. An apron made of heavy, beige colored cotton was wrapped around her skinny waist, and her hair was pulled back in a ponytail. Her persona reflected our sentiments to a T. She looked about thirty-something, but addressed us as though she were many years older.

"What'll you kids be having this morning?" she asked.

"I'll have the mushroom and cheese omelet with a glass of OJ, Debbie said respectfully, setting the menu back between the napkin holder, and salt and pepper shakers.

"I'll have two eggs over easy, some hash browns, bacon, wheat toast, a glass of chocolate milk and a small glass of OJ." I placed my menu back and I'm aware of Debbie looking my direction.

"Where do you put all that food? You gotta hollow leg or something?" she smirked. I shook my head in disbelief. Considering the way she is dressed, I found it preposterous she would be critical of me. I don't engage.

The waitress grinned at Debbie's humor, and turned to Patty, "and what would you like?"

Without looking at the menu Patty responded, "I'll have a bowl of oatmeal, and a cinnamon roll."

"Good for you," the waitress replied, "let me ask you again, what would you like from "this café?"

Debbie and I sat quietly, fascinated by the waitress's sarcasm. Patty, still not clear on the message, requested a bowl of frosted flakes, and a cup of coffee. The waitress shook her head from side to side; looked Patty dead in the eye, smiled, and said, "Now, when you came in, did you not see the sign out front?" Her condescending attitude toward Patty had Debbie, and me ready to implode.

"The one that said: no shirt, no shoes, no service?" Patty asked in a childlike manner.

"No, the other one," the waitress snarled. "The one that said the "**EGG**", she made the sign of quotations with her fingers, **"and I."** She leaned in close to Patty's face, and continued, "We don't serve pastries, flakes, toasties, loops, AND most of all oats."

Patty sat silently, unaffected by the waitress's sarcasm. She finally asked:

"Do you have cream and toast?"

"No."

"Yogurt?"

"No."

"Fruit?"

"What kind?"

"Peaches?"

"No."

"But you do have some fruit?"

"I have an apple in my lunch I'm willing to give up, so I can move on with my life," the waitress snickered, impressed at her joke.

"Ok, I'll have a hard-boiled egg, and some wheat toast, and a cup of coffee."

"Good for you, now you're catching on," the waitress remarked. She winked at Debbie, and me as she turned to leave and put our order in.

Patty was unstoppable, and proceeded to tell us about the kind of house that she was hoping to find when an annoying "MMMIIIAAA!" came screeching out of nowhere. We turned to see who was calling my name. I whispered "oh shit" under my breath, and Debbie mouthed "damn."

Approaching our table came one of the most beautiful women I'd ever met, beautiful only in the visual sense of the word. She had rich, chestnut brown hair, dimples on each side of a smile that held perfectly lined teeth, a tiny waist, and long shapely legs. Her biggest flaw was her appetite for booze, which led to a long list of undesirable men.

"Oh, hi Sharon," I said, trying not to sound too repulsed.

"You are sooo funny Mia," Sharon retorted condescendingly, "how many times do I have to tell you it's Jackal."

"I don't know, maybe a hundred," I said.

She sat on the vacant cane-back chair at our table for four, and horns in our privacy. "So, what immature shenanigans have you been up to since I moved out?" Without waiting for an answer, she continued, "Aren't you going to introduce me to your friends. Hi, I'm Jackal." She first extended her hand out to Patty.

Patty responded with a limp shake, and an obligatory "nice to meet you."

Sharon then turned to Debbie, extended her hand and said, "Hi, I'm Jackal." Debbie ignored her handshake and said, "We've met."

"We have? I don't remember," Sharon said.

Debbie's wit far exceeded Sharon's understanding, and responded with "No surprise there."

Ignoring Debbie's comment, Sharon continued with her inquisition. "So, what are you chicks up to?" she asked. Patty doesn't hesitate to seize the moment, filling Sharon in on her quest for the perfect home. Sharon pulled a nail file out of her purse, and began to smooth a snag on her index finger.

"Sounds utterly boring," she muttered, while dropping the file back in her purse. She slowly stood, and as though she looked down from an invisible pedestal, she leaned in with a whisper, "See you chicks later." Her strut had the cafés attention, as she made her exit.

"Who was that rude woman?" Patty asked with a sour look.

"An old nymphomaniac roommate" I answered.

CHAPTER EIGHTEEN

# PRINCE PLYMOUTH VALIANT

We finished breakfast and hopped in Patty's two-door, silver Nova. Debbie took the front passenger seat; I climbed in the back. Not really knowing what was in store for the day, Debbie asked Patty, "So, what's on the agenda besides driving around the neighborhood?"

"Well, we're meeting my realtor, Bobby Jones, at the first house, and then we'll follow him to the next one. He's very city knowledgeable, and also has an acute eye for detail, AND, a complete gentleman. Danny is very particular about whom I spend my time with. Especially if it's another man!" she giggled at the inference of being such a catch.

"So, we should probably be done around two?" I asked thinking it was a fair estimation.

"More like five," she said in all seriousness. "I'm free for the day, until I need to be home to cook for my husband of course." She made the next turn onto Bloomington Avenue.

"Oh, of course," Debbie started with her true-to-herself sarcasm. "How come you're not going to live at Danny's parents' place? A big horse ranch in Shakopee would be every woman's dream home."

70

"Danny's parents thought it would be a good experience to own our own home, before inheriting a thousand-acre ranch." Patty rambled on as though everyone born is faced with these same decisions.

She slowed the car down, and we saw a for sale sign in the front yard of a simple, but charming, bungalow. Its cream-colored stucco had an inviting quality with Scandinavian blue trim, and shutters. Delicate scalloped curtains could be seen through the windows, and a cord held a motionless pendulum from the half-drawn shades.

She pulled over to the curb, and parked behind a red 1964 Plymouth Valliant. Debbie was preoccupied; looking in her purse for a stick of gum. She'd been trying to quit smoking, and Patty's projected five o'clock finish time had exacerbated her withdrawal. Patty squealed, "Oh good, he's on time. I had to have a little 'talk to' with him, if you know what I mean." We don't, but she continued, "I'm a stickler on promptness and I hate waiting. He was ten minutes late for our appointment last time."

"Wow, ten whole minutes," Debbie said in a monotone voice, "I can't imagine such an atrocity."

Patty continued, "Now I know there are unexpected circumstances, and emergencies. Like for instance if he was thirty minutes late because of a flat, I could understand that. But ten minutes is just poor planning, and unacceptable." I fear if she keeps running off at the mouth, Debbie will lose her cool all together, and go for the choker again.

Bobby Jones stepped out of his car, and swaggered towards Patty, who was now standing outside the Nova. He was neatly dressed in black dress pants with wing tipped shoes. His white shirt, and black tie peeked out from under his dress coat. Debbie was still searching for her gum, and failed to notice the image of a very familiar individual. I, however, was familiar with the man I saw, and could barely speak. My vocal chords were temporarily fighting paralysis; a sinister laughter, and a thousand different scenarios dancing through my head; like the windows of a train speeding past me as I stood watching from the platform.

"Debbie," I managed to whisper.

"What?" she said without looking up from her purse.

"Debbie," I said as my vocals tried to reach a louder whisper.

"What!" she blurted and turned around from the front seat to look at me, annoyed by my conduct.

"Bobby Jones," I squeaked. She squinted at me in confusion.

Before closing the drivers' car door, Patty bent down and looked in at us, "Well? Are you two going to join us or not?" She giggled with excitement, and turned back to the courtesies of her realtor while slamming the door. Debbie looked out the front window and could only see the back side of Bobby Jones. His conservative afro told her he was black. Still nothing registered.

"What's the big deal?" Debbie asked me. "You act as if you've never seen a black man before."

Without another word, Debbie hopped out of the car. I did the same, but Bobby Jones was wholly engulfed with the attentions of Mrs. Chadwick, and without giving us a second glance the two of them had made their way to the front entrance of the house. I stared at Debbie waiting for her reaction, but her annoyance of the day's plans had her brooding, and she still hadn't acknowledged any connection with the Valiant and the realtor. Finally, she was awakened like a bear disrupted from winter hibernation. It was the sound of a familiar voice that made her come to life. She whirled around and gave the Valiant a familiar stare. Bobby Jones, still invested in his client's attention, was busy giving a dissertation on real estate:

"If you will notice the fine architecture, Mrs. Chadwick, and may I point out the fastidiousness in the placement of the windows. An astute builder I must say. It is imperative to comprehend the superiority of a well-crafted home, in the event of a natural catastrophe. You want to know you will be safe within its structure."

I'm thinking a natural catastrophe might happen at any moment. Patty giggled like a child, and was charmed by Bobby's terminology. Debbie, now alerted by the familiar tone of Bobby Jones, was resuscitated from her nicotine withdrawal by chewing rapidly on her stick of gum. Her eyes were wide open, and her complexion had taken on a full-bodied shade. She was calmer than I had expected, which was more unsettling than the contrary. She looked at me, and with a dead pan stare said, "Follow my lead." The thought of following her lead always frightened me, but I have no choice. I am the Novice, and she is my Mother Superior.

Bobby Jones unlocked the door, and held it open as Patty entered the threshold of her potential home. Like the gentlemen he was trying to be, he remained holding the door, and turned our direction nodding for us to enter. It was at that moment I believe his life flashed before him. His chocolate skin turned a shade of washed-out mahogany. He stared in disbelief at the flower child he once dated; she stared back at the masquerade of a businessman he was posing to be.

"Mr. Jones," Debbie greeted in all her beaded glamour, and walked slowly past him. He nodded in disbelief as her patchouli scent slapped him like wind chill out of the north. I followed her lead as instructed.

"Mr. Jones," I muttered holding back my laughter. It felt like slow motion walking passed the man Debbie and I knew as Renekee.

The first time I had met Renekee, he was wearing a long, brown suede coat, covering a paisley polyester shirt, bell bottom pants, and a huge afro with a hair pick anchored in the side. His idol was Jimmy Hendricks, and he did everything aesthetically possible to portray his appearance in rock star fashion. It was as far as he could go, considering he couldn't play a guitar, nor hold a tune. He had now traded in his paisley prints for starched white; comfortable bell bottoms for permanent press, polyester dress pants, and a haircut so short it wouldn't even hold a bobby pin. He followed trance-like behind me into the house, and we all gathered in the middle of the first room.

"I like what I see so far," Patty said as she gazed about the room. Renekee had lost all composure, and beads of sweat were appearing on his brow; he made no response, but stared at Debbie's lips as she spoke.

"What do you suppose the attic is like?" Patty's inquisition began, "the insulation I mean? You know how the Minnesota winters are. Gotta keep those fuel costs down."

"Well, let me look at the disclosure," Renekee stammered as he fumbled through the details of the home. "I'm sure it's up to code."

"Oh, I wouldn't trust that," Debbie smirked, "you should probably go up there and take a look. Don't you agree Mrs. Chadwick? Not everything makes it to the paper, if you know what I mean. Right Mr... what was your name again?"

"Oh Debbie, you're so perceptive. Yes, we better make sure before we go on any further. The last thing I want is a cold house." Patty chirped happily as she wondered in search of the door to the attic.

"It won't be a door Patty," said Debbie in a somewhat raised voice of authority, "this is a bungalow, you need to look for a hatch in the ceiling. Usually in an inconspicuous space, like maybe a closet."

Patty had gone wondering toward the back of the house, and Renekee took the opportunity to interrogate Debbie.

"What are you doing here?" he asked.

"I'm her friend."

"Why are you dressed like that?"

"I'm at peace with the universe."

"Why won't you return my calls?"

"What calls?"

"I leave messages with your mom every week."

"That's funny. She never told me a Bobby Jones called."

"I found it!" Pattie yelled, "I'm in the back bedroom. It's in the closet. A hatch in the ceiling just like you said."

## CHAPTER NINETEEN

# A CHANGE IN PLANS

**"I** didn't know Debbie could drive a stick, did you?" Patty asked as we followed Bobby Jones' Valiant down the street.

"She knows a lot of things," I replied, knowing Debbie was more than familiar with driving Renekee's car.

"I would have thought Bobby would have known the attic would have a low ceiling," Patty complained. "It's too bad we had to cancel my second appointment. For all I know, that could have been the house of my dreams, and all this searching would be over. Do you think he's ok?"

"I have to say, that was a pretty big bump on his head. I was really surprised how fast it popped up. I'm just glad he came to. It would have been really hard to get him out of the attic unconscious," I said.

"I didn't even see that nail sticking out from the side of the hatch. Did you? Pretty nasty rip in those pants. Do you think they were Oleg Cassini's?" Only Patty would give more thought to the condition of a pair of slacks rather than the blood it drew from scraping Renekee's leg.

"Yeah, he'll probably need a tetanus shot. Looked pretty rusty to me," I commented.

"Wow, Debbie's really going fast. I wonder if he's worse off than we think? He did hit the floor pretty hard coming down" Patty said.

"Tell me again why you needed to pull the ladder away from the hatch?" I asked.

"I wanted to measure the distance between the frame of the window, and the ceiling, in case I wanted to add crown molding. It just adds so much to a home you know. I was going to put it back. He said he had to rest a minute after bumping his head. I didn't know he was going to come down without warning," she justified.

"Too bad there wasn't shag carpet, it might have softened the blow when he landed" I said.

"True," said Patty, "but did you notice that the hard wood floors were in excellent condition? It was the best feature of the house, don't you think?"

We followed the Valiant up to the emergency room drop off; I hopped out of the Nova and ran inside to grab a wheel chair. When I returned Debbie was holding Renekee around the waist, and the two were leaned against the car.

"I can take it from here," Debbie said, "you and Patty can go home; I'll catch up with you at the flat."

"Gotcha", I winked, and got back in the Nova telling Patty we could leave.

"You mean she's staying with Bobby Jones?" Patty asked. "I guess I don't understand. He even leaned over and kissed her when you ran to get the wheel chair!"

"Some things in life just can't be explained, I guess that's kismet" I smirked, enjoying Patty's bit of confusion.

## CHAPTER TWENTY

# THE DATING GAME

The events that followed the house hunting fiasco were predictable. Debbie was trying her best not to be sucked back into Renekee's jive talking; smooth moving; romancing. But he was the best of the best, and she was charmed by his attentions. Something Revolution had been falling short on. Renekee had set up a date for the following Friday night. Revolution had a meeting with some fellow protestors, and Debbie opted out saying she and I were going to a movie. It wasn't completely a lie. She and I were going out, but on a double date. Renekee's best friend, Tom, said he would be thrilled to accompany me. Now one might say "Yay! Mia has a date," but truthfully, Tom was more of a warm body than a real live date.

Friday came, and it started to feel like old times as Debbie and I got ready. Let's face it, I had been living a pretty uneventful life since Revolution, and his followers swooped in, occupying our space, and my roommate's life. I wore my best jeans, tucking them into my knee high, fringed moccasins of course. I'm more excited to wear my new green, poor-boy sweater, than I am to be on a date. On weekends, I put away the electric rollers, and gave in to my natural curls. With some hairspray, and shaking my head up-side-down, I achieved the Janice Joplin effect. When Debbie started going for the natural look she'd been giving me her hand-me-down make-up. I had been studying the current styles in the fashion magazines, and how the models were enhancing their looks. I no longer resemble a country bumpkin, but rather a liberated city girl. We were ready early, and had some time to kill, so I turned on the TV, and took my position on the floor.

Every Saturday night you could find many households sitting in front of their televisions to watch "The Dating Game" shows. It had a reputation of saying things that slipped under the sensor of restrictions. The host of the show was Jim Lange, who introduced all the wanting bachelors, while the person seeking the date was off stage in a sound-proof booth. A split stage was decorated with a flower power design, and a comfortable chair waited on the left side of the partition for the person who would be asking the questions. Three tall director's chairs sat on the right side of the partition for the three bachelors, of which one would be chosen as the date. After announcing each bachelor's name, Jim described their occupation, hobbies and where they were from, as they smiled toward the camera: "Meet bachelor number one, Mark Martinson. He's a pig farmer from Kansas who likes hog calling, and sleeps in his birthday suit! Next we have bachelor number two, Jericho Peanut, from Little Rock, Arkansas. He is a mortician, and likes to be the life of the party! And last, but not least, we have bachelor number three, Norman Coats from Nashville, Tennessee. He's an actor, and hopes to be discovered some day. His favorite pass time is looking in the mirror!" The TV audience applauds, and then stops abruptly. Without hesitation, he introduces the woman who is hoping to meet the perfect date, and give a brief introduction.

"Please welcome Tally Hoe! She's a cocktail waitress from Palm Beach, Florida. She holds a Bachelor's teaching degree in Science, Math, and English but couldn't survive on a teacher's salary, and now works as an exotic dancer!" The woman was equipped with relevant questions for the bachelors to answer, to decide whom, she will pick for her date. Will it be bachelor number one, number two, or number three? All this may seem a bit boring, until they have a contestant with quick wit.

Woman: "Bachelor number one, describe your heritage in 20 words or less."

Bachelor number one: "My mother was Welsh, my father was Hungarian, and that makes me Well-Hung."

The woman is repulsed by his answer, and her upper lip curls a bit. The camera quickly switched to Jim, who was at a loss for words.

Woman: "Bachelor number two, what do you like best about your current occupation?"

Bachelor number two: "My clients usually agree with everything I say."

The woman smiled, and gave a childish giggle, and said, "Bachelor number three, what is your best feature?"

Bachelor number three: "I believe my left side."

The woman reacted as though she had found the perfect match, and said, "That's my best feature too!"

Bachelor Number Three was picked. He patiently waited until the two unwanted bachelors walked around the partition, meeting the girl they might have had a date with, but for some reason beyond their grasp, didn't get picked. Then, the final moment in the show had arrived. The winning bachelor who sat alone, and smiled like he just won the lottery, was asked to "Come and meet your date!"

Trumpets started playing a Herb Alpert tune, and the bachelor stood up from the chair without one wrinkle in his leisure suit. His high-top shoes looked out of place with the length of his pants. His glasses were kind of thick, and his hair was long with mutton chops hitting his jaw line. Tally Hoe was wearing a spandex mini dress with white plastic pearls, and chunky, open toed heals. She had a pretty face with way too much mascara, and glossy lipstick. She bounced a little with excitement and her forty D bust line jiggled, sending Jim's eyes rolling in his head. The dater and the datee met at last, and they simultaneously turned so their left sides were facing the camera. Jim explained with great enthusiasm as to what the date was that "The Dating Game" had arranged.

"We are sending you to Disneyland!" Jim almost yells in his emcee voice, "You will get to meet Donald Duck, and Mickey Mouse! You will have dinner at Sleeping Beauty's Castle! And you'll top off the night watching fireworks from the balcony of your adjoining hotel rooms!"

The couple looked at each other, and caressed as though it was meant to be, and it would be the greatest time of their life, but quickly reposition so their left sides were in view of the camera.

I feared Debbie and I were going out with a pig farmer, and mortician duplicates.

Renekee, who was once habitually late, arrived ten minutes early. Debbie had me answer the door so she could make her entrance at the appropriate moment, and she disappeared quickly into our bedroom. I answered the door.

Renekee gave me a nod as he entered, and walked into our living room. Tom followed closely behind, pausing momentarily in the doorway smiling. "Hello Mia," he said softly. I had no clever greeting, and stood speechless. Tom was tall, and slender with sandy blonde hair cut in a shag style, and wore wire rimmed glasses. When I had first met him, about a year ago, he had scruff where a mustache should be. But now it was filled in adding fetching richness to his looks. He wore a coat made popular by a cigarette company, over a cashmere, black turtleneck. His blue jeans, that were at one time faded, are now creased, dark indigo. His smile was still mischievous and I'm pleasantly surprised.

"Where's Debbie?" Renekee asked.

"Still getting ready, she'll be out soon."

"What's that shit on the windows?"

"Curtains."

"What am I smelling?"

"Incense."

"What's with all the rope?"

"It's macramé."

"Are you two doing drugs?"

"No."

"Whose idea was it for the hanging beads?"

"Ours, how's your head?"

"Hurts a little, three stitches."

"What about the leg?"

"A pain in my ass from the tetanus shot."

Tom stood smiling, enjoying the banter between his friend, and me. Debbie finally made her entrance, and said "If you're done with your interrogation we can go."

I'm amusingly surprised by her change in wardrobe. She had pitched the tie-dyed shirt, and macramé vest for a tight fitting black turtleneck. Her lashes were now enhanced with black mascara, and her lips boasted a deep pink shade. Renekee was delighted at what he saw, and started with a compliment, or at least tried.

"Well, my, my, you are one fine looking woman. I have to admit, I wasn't sure if you were going to look like a hippy chic, but I was willing to overlook it".

Sometimes men just don't know when not to talk; Renekee was one of them.

"Are you still at peace with the universe?" He grinned, impressed with himself at pushing the envelope. Tom quietly snickered at his friends' behavior.

"With the universe yes," Debbie said, "With you? I'm not so sure."

## CHAPTER TWENTY-ONE

# REIGNITING THE FLAME

**"S**o, what's the plan?" Renekee asked.

"You're asking me?!" Debbie retorted.

"Just shittin' ya woman," Renekee grinned with a wink, and Debbie blushed realizing he knew just how to push her buttons.

"Here is our plan for the night," Renekee continued as we all intently listened. "First, we need to grab some grub. I reserved us a table at the Spaghetti House down town. Then we'll take in the nine o'clock show at the Avalon. Have you seen Love Story yet?"

"No, but I'd like to," Debbie said, charmed by his well thought plan for the evening.

"Good. Then after the movie, we'll wrap up the night at the Rainbow for some desert. I requested a table by the window," he said.

"You can't make reservations at the Rainbow, they don't take reservations," Debbie commented.

*On the corner of Lake Street and Hennepin Avenue sits the Rainbow Café, one of the largest family restaurants in the Twin Cities, hosting a variety of clientele. Cozy naugahyde booths lined the perimeter, and paintings by local artists hung on the walls, adding a classy esthetic favorable to the elderly and socialites. They were all for sale, and were often purchased by the avant-garde collector. There were over fifty galleries in the city, but the Rainbow Café offered an artist the opportunity to sell their creations without paying a commission. It was an artist's dream to have a work of art hang in the Rainbow, where the flow of spectators was never ending.*

*The waitresses all had silver hair, and a story to tell. Their name tags of Mable, Alvina, Dorothy, and Rose spoke of days gone by. Their uniforms were a traditional black, shirt-waist dress, short sleeves with white cuffs, and a white collar. Staying open, until the late-night hours, gave venue to theatre goers. Women with mink pillbox hats, cashmere coats, and pocketbooks hanging in the crux of one arm could be seen holding onto their partner, usually a man dressed in a tweed overcoat, balancing his posture with a cane of mahogany and pewter entering for a late-night snack. Due to the restaurants popularity, reservations were never taken at the Rainbow.*

"Baby," Renekee said, "I got the right connections, you'll see."

When we got to the Spaghetti House our dates were complete gentlemen. Renekee opened doors, Tom was pulling out chairs. The night was missing the usual antics between the two men, but we were enjoying the special treatment. Renekee was filling us in on how he got involved in real estate, why he cut his Hendrix hair, and what he wishes to achieve in life. Tom was busy eating, agreeing, and smiling. He didn't contribute much to the conversation, but I had guessed there had been changes in his life considering his mature selection of clothes, and his well-groomed appearance.

Renekee left a substantial tip for our waiter, and said now that he had a professional man's income he would be giving back to those in need. Debbie was enamored by his generosity, Tom was oblivious, and I was enjoying our night out, tip or no tip.

We headed over to the Avalon Theatre, and the guys bought our tickets, and candy: Jordan Almonds for me, and Milk Duds for Debbie. Tom and Renekee passed on the candy, and each got a coke. We took our seats in the middle row in the center of the theatre, and before the movie started Renekee was already holding Debbie's hand. Tom and I sat like strangers, which was fine by me. I liked Tom, but I really didn't know much about him. He wasn't much for conversation, and was mostly a side kick to Renekee. I had no idea of what he liked to do, if he had a job (although I assume he did), or where he went to school. These are things we should have talked about, if we were dating, but we're not. The first time I met Tom was actually on New Year's Eve. It was a similar scenario, he was with Renekee, and I was with Debbie. We were driving down the road, and there they were looking under the hood of Renekee's car that wouldn't start. Before the night was over, Renekee and Debbie were having one of their classic lovers' quarrels, and Tom and I were standing in the cold of a winters night looking up at a black sky feeling the snow fall on our faces. The church bells in the city rang in the New Year, and Tom kissed me like I'd never been kissed before. I know I haven't been kissed like that since, and I wondered if he remembered the moment like I did, or if it was just routine, and no big deal to him. Part of me would like to have a replay, but my candor stopped me from sending any signals to the like.

"Love Story," was a sad, sad movie. I held back my tears when Jenny Cavalleri lay in the hospital bed during her last hour of life. I glanced to my left at Tom, and he had no reaction to the scene, just kept sipping his coke. I looked to my right, and Debbie was burying her head in Renekee's shoulder, sobbing as he comforted her. It occurred to me that this was Renekee's well thought out plan all along. I'm all for it, anything to get Revolution out of my friend's life.

After the movie, we headed over to the Rainbow Café; it was packed with the usual late night Uptown crowd piling in for their late-night nibbles. Debbie commented, "We'll have to wait forever."

Renekee pulled her in close, and whispered in her ear, "Baby, I told you I have connections."

We got up to the hostess stand, and the manager said, "Renekee my man! How was the show?"

"Show was good dude," Renekee answered, and then asked "you have that table ready?"

"Yes sir, right this way," the manager nodded and we followed him to a table set for four, next to the window looking out at Lake Street.

Debbie and I were impressed, and gave each other a glance of approval. We took our seats, and began to look over the menu. Renekee said he's having cheese cake; Debbie goes with apple pie; I've decided on a hot fudge sundae. We are waiting for Tom, whose head was still hidden in the menu.

"Dude?" asks Renekee.

Tom didn't respond.

"Dude!" Renekee said again, "do you know what you want?"

Tom burst into tears; big crocodile tears. His face was beat red, and he reached for several napkins out of the dispenser. He could barely speak, but tried between the sobs, "I think I'll go with the fudge cake. Blaaaaaaaa," he cried inconsolably.

"Dude?" Renekee asked, "What's got you down man?"

Tom continued, "Why did she have to die….why…I mean, it must have been really hard to get into Radcliff. And her dad….poor guy…raising her on his own….and what about Oliver's dad…he was so mean…..couldn't he have been just a little bit nicer…..whaaaaaa."

Debbie, and I sat surprised at Tom's delayed reaction of the movie.

"Pull it together man, it's just a movie. They're just actors, you dig?" Renekee tried to calm him down, and it was becoming embarrassing with all the attention Toms sobs were drawing to our table.

"You're right man….just lost my grip," Tom blubbered. He picked up his wad of tear soaked napkins, and blew his nose with a sound very similar to a deflating balloon. He gave me an uncomfortable grin, and I felt the need to reassure him.

"I think its sweet….really," I said. "I get emotional too sometimes. Like the time my brother, and I were kids, and we were playing cowboys and Indians. Well, we were up in the barn haymow, and I was hiding behind some hay bales. My brother had a lasso, of course he was the cowboy, and I was the Indian. Actually, I was probably Pocahontas. Anyway, he was supposed to capture me, but instead our cat came out of nowhere and ran in front of my brother. He impulsively lassoed it! That might have been ok, but the cat got scared, and took off running in the wrong direction, and fell down the hatch. So, what does my brother do, but yank it back up. Well, that was the end of the cat. Busted its….."

"We get it Pocahontas!" Debbie shrieked, shooting me a scowl.

"I'm only trying to explain to Tom that I understand when emotions hit. After that happened I couldn't stop crying for hours, until my dad dug a hole; we buried the cat with a graveside service."

"I don't think I can take another farm story," Debbie moaned.

"You act like I talk about the farm all the time? When was the last time I told a farm story?" I refuted.

"Yesterday," she said, "when you gave me your thesis on how to cook venison, so the tallow doesn't coat the roof of your mouth."

"Fine." I grunted.

We finished our deserts, and headed back to the flat. Renekee ended the night with a kiss for Debbie. Tom and I smiled awkwardly at each other, and I told him I had fun.

"Me too," he said, and gave me a hug. All in all, bachelors one, and three proved to be winner status.

## CHAPTER TWENTY-TWO

# LUTHER BENSON

Lake Phalen was a long, narrow body of water that was perfect for ice skating, and a picturesque backdrop for Winter Carnival events. Eight years ago, Sven Karleen had moved to St. Paul from International Falls, where it was winter almost nine months a year. He was svelte, and fit as a fiddle. He had been ice skating since he was old enough to walk, and considered it a form of relaxation. When he first attended the Lake Phalen skating event, as a spectator, he had asked a fellow standing next to him (with his heavy Scandinavian accent), "Why are they going so slow? Don't they want to win the race?"

That fellow happened to be Gunner Bjorkman, the most sought-after coach in the twin cities, who'd been working with the skater leading the race. Sven's heavy accent immediately got Gunners attention. He turned to Sven, and with a cynical tone asked, "Do you think you could do better my friend?"

"Ya, sure, I know I could," Sven answered.

After the race Gunner and Sven went for a cup of coffee, and a long conversation. From that point on it was history in the making for the two of them. Sven would win the race at Lake Phalen for the next eight years.

Last year, when Sven turned 50, everyone was sure it would be the year he would lose to the young, Luther Benson. Luther was in his twenties, and had been training all year for the event, succeeding in all local races. Behind the scenes everyone was placing bets against Sven, figuring the old timer was sure to be beaten; Luther had his youth and the muscle to win.

On the night before the event Luther went to the North Star Stadium, and approached a man named Zeke, who drove the Zamboni. It cost a lot of money for ice time, and Luther figured he could bribe Zeke into letting him practice by slipping him a couple of bucks under the table. Zeke didn't care for Luther's condescending attitude. He told Luther, "You might think you're big stuff around here, but I'm in charge of the ice rink, and locking up the stadium."

"I meant no disrespect, I just thought you could use a few extra bucks, and I could use a little practice on my curves," said Luther.

Zeke was a small-framed man; standing at about 5' 2" with his boots on. He hated the way the big shot skaters would come around acting like they were better than him. Zeke removed his glove from his right hand, and stroked his chin as he stared up at Luther. "Come to think of it," he said, "I could use some extra cash." Luther followed up with two fives and smirk.

Zeke was in control now. "You got one hour. No more," he ordered. Zeke then left without any further conversation. Locking all but one door on his way out; he made note of Luther's shiny, new MG sitting under the parking lot flood lights. "Spoiled little jerk," he muttered to himself. He then hopped in his old, rusted out Ford pickup, and headed out of the lot thinking a beer at O'Rileys Pub sounded good.

When Zeke arrived at the pub all the talk was about the next day's race. The bartender was taking bets, and the odds were 4 to 1 that Luther had it in the bag. Now Zeke wasn't highly educated, but he knew a good thing when he saw it. This could be pay dirt for him in more ways than one. He ordered an Old Milwaukee, and laid his paycheck on the bar. "I'd like to put it all on "Sven Karleen," Zeke said with a smile.

"You mean on Luther, dontcha bud?" the bartender asked, as he looked at Zeke perplexed.

"Nope. Put the money on Sven," Zeke repeated with a nod.

Zeke drank his beer, and with the hour almost up, headed back to the North Star Stadium to lock up. A light snow was starting to fall, and sparkling crystals were collecting on the only car in the North Star lot. Zeke drove slowly past Luther's MG, and pulled up to the one entrance that remained unlocked. He hopped out of his truck, leaving the motor running, walked over to the door and slipped in his key, turning the bolt lock. Feeling light on his feet, he returned to his truck, and slowly rumbled past the MG on his way out of the parking lot.

The next day Luther Benson never showed for the competition. Sven Karleen won his last race, and retired. The Winter Carnival board ignored Luther's claims of sabotage, telling Luther he was "making excuses," and "was too big for his britches," and "a bad sport."

Zeke collected his winnings, and left for a well-deserved vacation.

## CHAPTER TWENTY-THREE

# PLACE YOUR BETS

I called my high school friend, Finbar MacMaolduin, and made a date to meet him Saturday morning at the Normandy Inn Kitchen Restaurant, in downtown Minneapolis. Finbar was the class president back in high school, and we barely looked at each other then. But happenstance literally made us run into each other about a year ago. We've been good friends ever since. His physical appearance wasn't exactly my type. He was six feet tall with red hair, and prominent freckles. He was pretty shy when it came to conversing with the opposite sex, but I managed to bring him out of his shell. We tried dating once, but then decided we were better suited as friends. Finbar wanted a career, wife, and kids. I didn't know what I wanted, but I was definitely not ready to travel down any domesticated road just yet. His classes at Macalester College were pretty demanding, so we hadn't seen each other for some time. I was excited we were finally getting together.

I arrived early, and slipped into a leather booth, next to the window. The Kitchen was an inviting place with warm colors of red, tieback curtains, and mahogany wood tables. I ordered some hot cocoa, and asked the waitress to bring another when my friend arrived. Cupping my hands around the warm cup, I blew gently against the steam, letting it warm my face.

Saturday's were quiet downtown. Very little traffic passed by the window, as I stared out at the city that was once again shadowed by clouds, and a light flurry of snow. A tall figure of a man appeared down the block, approaching in my direction with a stride that was risky for the slick sidewalks. His cap and scarf were covering most of his face, but I knew it was Finbar. He saw me in the window, and waved as he did a side slide to The Kitchen's entrance.

Not paying any attention to the snow that had collected on his boots, coat, and hat; he made a bee line to where I was waiting. I quickly stood to give him a hug, and he hugged me back lifting me off the floor. It felt nice until we were both struck with an uncomfortable self-consciousness. Too much affection for "friend" standards. His good nature, as always, was revealed with eyes that danced. He didn't seem as skinny as he was in high school, or when I last saw him. His shoulders had gotten a little broader, and I felt solid arms when we hugged.

"Wow! It's good to see you!" Finbar said. He removed his stocking cap and scarf, allowing soft red curls to fall to his shoulders.

"Your hair!" I exclaimed.

"Yeah, isn't it long? At first, I stopped going to the barber to save money. Then I realized it was kinda keeping my head warm for the winter, so I just let it grow. You dig?"

I smiled, "I dig."

For Finbar to use the term, dig, told me he had broadened his circle of friends, going beyond the scholarly. The waitress brought a cup of cocoa for Fin, and we ordered four popovers, three for Fin, and one for me. Conversation flowed easily between us. We covered all the generalities of our daily lives, my job, his school, then Fin asked:

"So, how's everything working out with you, and Debbie as roommates?"

"It could be better that's for sure. She kind of went all bohemian on me." I continued to explain how Debbie's encounter with the flower people was accidental, but intrusive. I continued on about the contrast between Revolution, and Renekee, and how Debbie seemed to be under Revolutions spell.

"No kidding. I guess I can't say that I saw that coming. I figured Debbie to be too city-chic to go the hippy route. Too fashion conscious. I always relate that hippy movement with dirt, and marijuana. Like planting stuff, and living in an old farmhouse that's been sitting on forty acres in the middle of nowhere. Maybe a house that belongs to a family whose parents are now dead, and the siblings are grown up, and in an argument. They can't agree on selling their childhood home. Half want to keep it, and the other half wants to sell it. Maybe it will cost a lot of money to maintain, and they're too cheap to fix it up. There are leaks in the roof, and the front porch is rotted. So, they rent it out to a bunch of nonconformists who want to lay around all day, smoke pot, and have sex with whomever happens to be in bed next to them. They go under the façade of being a commune; when in reality they're a bunch of lazy ass kids that don't want to grow up. They have one car, a station wagon. The women stay at the farm doing things like trying to figure out how to use the old wringer washer, chopping wood for the wood burning stove, and doing macramé. The men go into town, and make a few bucks doing day labor. They get a couple of goats to mow the yard, and have this idea in their feeble heads that they will sell goats milk. One day they wake up, and can't figure out where the goats disappeared to, even though they didn't put up fences. Their running water comes from an old pump, and they use little electricity in hopes to keep the cost down. They resort to burning candles, and the princess curtains, that had remained for when mom and pop were alive, go up in flames. They put the fire out, but they now have singed wall paper that is beginning to flake from the walls. There is only one toilet that was installed in what was once a pantry in the kitchen; so, if you have to do your "business" you need to take it outside to the outhouse. It's easier to bath in a lake than filling the galvanized tub, and using a heating element to bring the temperature up to a mere sixty degrees. Then one of the girls ends up pregnant. She doesn't know who the father is, and starts looking at the calendar in hopes of figuring it out. None of the guys step up to the plate, claiming they're not ready for commitments, and tell her she should have been taking the pill. But how can she take "the pill" when it goes against their free life style. She realizes she's made a mess of her life, and packs her belongings of an extra sack dress, and two pairs of socks in a satchel, and hitch hikes home. Then one day her parents see her walking up the driveway with a baby in her belly, due to pop out any day. Yep, I just can't picture Debbie going down that road."

"Wow, Finbar! Is that what you're learning in your humanities class?" I asked, impressed with his grasp on the human condition.

"No, it's my sister."

"Oh crap, I'm speechless."

"You're speechless? My parents couldn't talk for three days! Maybe Debbie will come to her senses before it's too late. I have to say, I really didn't see that coming… with her."

"Trust me, neither did I. Maybe there's hope now that Renekee's reentered her life," I said, hoping my words were gospel.

Our popovers arrived, and we took in a deep breath, inhaling the aroma of the fresh baked pastry. Finbar had a large plate to accommodate three, and mine was on a smaller desert plate. Steam escaped as we pulled them open, and we quickly spread whipped almond butter in the center.

"Are you going to the race at Phalen?" Finbar asked, with a little bit of butter escaping out of the corner of his mouth.

"Actually, it's the one event I don't want to miss. In fact, Debbie said she wanted to go with me. Of course, there is always the possibility of Revolution spoiling our plan."

"Wanna make some money on it?"

"On what? What are you talking about?"

"Well, words out around campus that Luther Benson's gonna throw the race."

"What! How come?"

"He's still ticked off about last year's race, still claiming it was sabotage. He wants to stick it to the establishment, so I hear. I guess he'll make more money by being crooked. I've never met the guy, but I hear he's kind of a jerk."

"How do you know all this?" I asked, taking my last bite of popover; wishing I had ordered two.

"At the dorm we call it classified information." Finbar took on an authoritative persona. "One of the guys at the dorm has an uncle that's a bookie. As it stands right now, the odds-on Luther are two to one, BUT, Victor Kotny is the second favorite, with odds on him being ten to one. So, if the rumor is true you can make a hundred dollars with ten bucks."

"Finbarr! I never thought of you as a gambler."

"College has corrupted me, what can I say," he grinned.

I'd planned to pick up some groceries on my way home, but decided that could wait. I still had a half jar of peanut butter, and four slices of bread. I gave Finbarr a ten spot, and we hugged goodbye.

## CHAPTER TWENTY-FOUR

# OVERTIME

The days were always so short in the winter. I left for work in the dark, and by the time I had returned home it was dark once again. The lack of sunshine made me tired, and riding the bus home was comparable to a ship at sea. Each time the bus stopped to pick up new passengers it rocked its cargo forward like waves hitting shore. Heads would bob forward, as shoulders followed briefly. As the mighty ship forged on, leaving the stop, the waves forced our shoulders back. Instinctively we braced for our nodding heads. No one talked after a long day at work. We rode in silence, inhaling exhaust fumes that escaped through the floor, hoping to reach our destination before becoming totally asphyxiated. I feared someday I would fall asleep, miss my stop, and be stuck on the never-ending bus ocean.

I had worked late doing inventory, and didn't catch the 17 until almost 7 o'clock. A different group of people were riding at this hour, with no familiar faces of the nine to fivers. I grabbed the last seat at the back of the bus next to the window, setting my purse in the vacant seat next to me. It was bitter cold outside; but the bus blasted its heat, making a warm respite for its travelers. I closed my eyes, trying not to give in to my exhaustion. Only eight more blocks until Garfield Avenue.

I felt the bus stop again to take on more passengers. "Is this seat taken?" a man's voice asked with a sophisticated tone.

"No," I said. Placing my purse on my lap, I opened my eyes to peek at who spoke. He must have been close to six feet tall, but he sat down before I could get a good estimate. His eyes were gentle, and looked hazel colored in the dim light. His lips were full, and his high cheekbones were framed by his sorrel colored hair that fell like the mane of a stallion. His complexion was pocked, but it didn't interfere with his impressive looks. I guessed him to be in his thirties, too old for me to take a second look.

"Do you ride this bus often? I don't remember seeing you before." He spoke quietly as if he might disturb those around us.

"I usually take an earlier one," I answered. Unwilling to continue the small talk, I was too nervous to look him in the eye. I stared into the window catching his reflection.

"Must have been a long day for you," he said apologetically.

I closed my eyes for moment, listening to him continue about his day. When I open to catch another look at him, he was gone. Everyone was gone, except for the bus driver who knelt in my direction on the seat in front of me.

"Young lady you've been sleeping back here for most of my shift; I think you missed your stop." He gave me an unintentional wink, "I've been watching yak; making sure nobody bothers ya. Folks are safe on my route." He seemed genuine, in a grandfather sort of way. "It's midnight, no busses running now for the next three hours."

"Shit," I whispered, and caught a look of disapproval from my self-appointed bodyguard.

"I'll call you a cab" he said.

## CHAPTER TWENTY-FIVE

# THE RACE IS ON

**D**ebbie and I had agreed to meet at Lake Phalen, fifteen minutes before race time. Even though she'd gone out with Renekee, she still wasn't sure she wanted to end things with Revolution. She had spent last night at Revolutions, but fortunately he had things to do today. To my relief, he wasn't going to interfere with our day.

It was a sunny, balmy day with virtually no wind; perfect for racing. I felt good, and ready for a day of fresh air, and if luck would have it, making a hundred bucks. The ice track was a quarter mile oval with four rounded, but risky corners. The skaters would have to make four rounds to complete the mile race. Poles were placed every twelve feet around the circumference of the rink, and a rope swaged between them, making a boundary line for spectators. Debbie and I had agreed to meet at the third corner of the track.

I arrived a bit early, so I could secure a good vantage point. As I waited the crowd started to build, but I was sure Debbie would have no problem working her way through the many observers. I checked out the people on the opposite side of the track, in hopes I might see Finbarr when Debbie's voice came from behind me.

"Man, it's colder than a witch boob out here," she exclaimed.

"It's tit... colder than a witch's tit." I said without looking, and then turned to greet her. I hadn't given much thought to what Debbie would be wearing. After her date with Renekee I just assumed her real self was going to resurface.

"Oh....Hi," I said trying not to look surprised. However, I was perplexed as to what to say next. Debbie's hair was stuffed under a yellow, wool knit hat, most likely made by Cosmic River, or Hyacinth. It had triangular earflaps with long braided ties, to resemble Nordic hair. Instead of the green army coat, she now wore a sheep skin number with wavy tufts of fur exploding from the seams, and lots of embroidery swirling about. Her clogs helped her gain back some of the height she'd lost with her deflated hair style, but a scowl still hovered over her brow. This once magnetic fashion plate had converted to the floundering antithesis of a Viking archetype.

"What are you staring at?" she snarled at me.

"Nothing, don't be so defensive," I said.

"I'm not. You're giving me that look of disapproval." She had lapsed back to her argumentative peace-loving Revolution protégé.

"I'm not, really, this is my face, can't change it." I was irritated by her accusation, and my sarcasm flowed easily. When Debbie reconnected with Renekee, there was a glimmer of hope. One night with Revolution, and she was lost in his power again. Luckily, I'm saved from any further confrontation by a gunshot echoing through the trees. The race was on.

There were eight contestants who made it into the final race. Like horses out of the gate, they were all progressing at the same speed on the first round. By the second round three were lagging behind, and Luther Benson, and Victor Kotny were in the top five. Third time around Luther Benson was four lengths ahead of Victor Kotny, and I'm thinking I should have kept my ten dollars. The crowd began cheering, and screaming Luther's name. He was gaining to where I knew there was no hope of Victor winning. They were on the fourth and last round; Luther's skates barely hit the ice, and he was flying like a bird, as he approached the third and last corner.

Within a split second all hell broke loose, sending the crowd in a loud gasp. Luther's feet flew out from under him, landing him on the left side of his buttocks. He spun an unbelievable horizontal triple salchow, heading our direction at lightning speed. Before anyone could run for cover, Luther slid under the rope crashing into several people in his wake. He hit Debbie like the front pin of a strike, sending her clogs airborne, and her arms flailing. The crowds' audible horror made it so I could only lip read the four-letter words Debbie was spewing vehemently. She landed with a thud. I quickly rushed to her side, and knelt down next to her.

"Are you ok?!" I ask panicking, worried that she was seriously hurt.

"What just happened?! I think somethings wrong with my ankle," she winced. She tried to stand but the pain was too much.

"I can give you a ride to the hospital," Finbar said, "I have my dad's car."

"Finbar!" I gasped, "Wow, where'd you come from?"

"I was about sixty feet down. When I saw what happened I ran up to check out Luther, but he had already got up and split. I didn't know you were standing here until just a moment ago."

"Hey, I'm in pain here!" Debbie howled.

Debbie was the only casualty left by Luther, except for an innocent snow goose getting bopped by a flying clog. The other spectators that were knocked over managed to leave the scene unscathed. Finbar and I cut our conversation short, and hoisted Debbie off of the snow. We each took an arm, helping her hobble on one leg to Finbar's car. Next stop: St. Joseph's ER.

## CHAPTER TWENTY-SIX

# CANDY STRIPER SHE'S NOT

We arrived at St. Joseph's, and Debbie was put in a wheelchair at the door. Finbar waited until we were escorted to an area where rows of beds were surrounded by curtains.

"I think I'm gonna book. I'll catch up with you later this week, once I pick up our money." Finbar's smile widened with a little naughty look.

"Money! You mean Victor Kotny won?!" I blurted, briefly forgetting my surroundings, and hospital etiquette.

Finbar winked, and replied like a true Scandinavian, "You betcha".

I was filling in the blanks for Debbie, when a nurse popped into our curtain room, and began taking Debbie's vitals, and said she was going to take her down to X-ray. At Debbie's request, I needed to find a pay phone and call Revolution to ask him to come to the hospital. I agreed to meet Debbie back at the curtain room. When we all returned the nurse helped Debbie into the hospital bed, and told us the doctor would be by soon. She then smiled at me, assuring me my friend was going to be fine. "She's been given something for the pain, and will be feeling a little sleepy," she informed me.

"Did you reach him?" Debbie garbled.

"No answered, I called Renekee, he's on his way."

"I guess we won't be going to the Castle lighting ceremony tonight." Debbie sighed, "I'm sorry."

"It's ok, too cold anyway," I said.

The pain medication had taken over, and she didn't hear my answer. Sitting in an emergency room on a sunny Saturday afternoon wasn't what I'd expected to be doing. But then again, it was never what I expected when Debbie and I hung out. I pulled the curtain back so I could do a little people watching while Debbie dozed. I pushed my steel folding chair up to the one wall in our tiny space, and tried to get comfortable. I slid down about halfway on the seat, so I could lean my head back, resting against the grey plaster wall. The ER was all a-bustle with doctors being called over the intercom. A code blue alerted the staff to someone a couple of curtain rooms away.

I closed my eyes, and imagined I was a prize in a Monty Hall game show, and he'd given the doctors their choice of what was behind curtain number one, two, or three. A familiar voice startled me from my daydream bringing me back to reality, presenting me the proverbial topping on the cake of irony for the day.

"Mia, is that you?" Her voice was shrill, and all too familiar. My past flashed before me, and reluctantly I opened my eyes.

*And what to my wondering eyes should appear, but an old roommate in janitorial gear.*

"Phyllis? Phyllis Alby?"

Her powdery scent took over the curtain room in a matter of seconds. I wanted to gag. Although she wore glasses, a silver chain still hung onto them, swooping down, and around the back of her neck, like reins on a mare. Her loud squawk of laughter made Debbie's eyes flutter, even under sedation. She had put on weight since I had seen her last. However, her grey uniform camouflaged it well, but her full cheeks told the true story.

"What happened to your friend?" Phyllis asked, nodding toward Debbie.

"Long story… Do you work here?" I asked.

"I like to think of it as a temporary solution to my financial enigma. God knows I'm meant for more important positions." She made the sign of the cross.

Typical answer, Phyllis was always placing her lack of honesty on the fault of others, and turning religious when it suited her. When we were roommates she was arrested in a raffle ticket scam, and lost her prestigious job at Dayton's Oval Room. Back then her son Christopher was about to be sprung from Stillwater State Penitentiary. I was relieved when she was asked to leave the place we rented on Freemont. From the stories Phyllis had told me, Christopher was someone I would never want to meet. When we parted ways, I had hoped it was the last I would see of her.

"So, how's Christopher?" Why I asked, I don't know. I knew I'd regret it.

"Oh, you know Christopher, never easy with that boy." Phyllis always spoke of Christopher as though he was barely twelve years old. She forever made excuses for his apprehensible behavior. Phyllis continued, as if I hadn't heard enough.

"He hooked up with some slut, and she has turned him against me. He never visits me. And to think I spent every Sunday at Mass praying for his release; every Sunday afternoon, my only day off mind you, at the prison; sitting on a hard metal chair, just to visit him on the other side of a glass window! And for what? To be treated like an inconvenience. Cast aside like an old shoe. To be told to mind my own business!" Phyllis shook her head as she dusted her way around the curtain room. "And to think I named him a good, Catholic name like Christopher!" She tilted her head forward, and peered at me over the frame of her glasses. "It means 'Christ-like' you know... and now that slut has convinced him to change it!"

"Really, to what?" I asked.

"Tyrone, as in Guthrie. He said it carried more prestige. Humph, as if he would know about prestige."

"Oh." I knew what I needed to ask next, and feared I already knew what the answer would be. Her continuous talking irritated me like traffic noise, but I tried to muster up as much nonchalance as possible.

"So, what's the slut's name?" I asked, fearing what the answer might be.

"Bonita," she grumbled.

## CHAPTER TWENTY-SEVEN

# THE CASTLE

Although the Winter Carnival was only a two-week event, construction of the Ice Castle began the day after New Year's, to be completed by the opening day of the festivities. Its appearance resembled many a fairy tale fashion, with a draw bridge extending over a mote of ice and snow. Extravagant ice sculptures of swans, and unicorns were placed around the perimeter of the ice-block rooms, and turrets. Lighting was strategically placed with all cords buried under the snow, to carry out the mysterious illusion of a story book land. After weeks of volunteers embracing the elements, by wearing layers of long johns, wool shirts, and dungarees, the task was completed, and ready for guests.

On the night of the lighting ceremony, a small stage was constructed in front of the castle, by the draw bridge. St. Paul's Mayor, and other city dignitaries, were present. Local news teams were summoned to tape the event, which would later be broadcasted on the 10PM news. A small crowd, of mostly women, had gathered. They wore heavy overcoats, mittens, and crocheted hats with matching scarves wrapped around their necks, and faces. Only their eyes could be seen peeking out into the bitterness. Boots crunched, and squeaked as they walked across the snow, following a trail marked by posts with ribbon swaged between them. Taking their places in front of the make shift podium, they waited while the Mayor stepped up to the microphone, cleared his throat, and started by thanking everyone for coming.

The news stations were set up close to the podium, focused on the Mayor. The women were starting to get cold, and began stomping their feet, and flapping their arms trying to keep the adrenalin flowing. One police car had rolled by out of curiosity. There had never been a need for police patrol in all the years of the Winter Carnival. After a quick look, the confident squad car continued on its way without noticing the suspicious group of young people dressed in army surplus attire. They had discretely hidden their protest signs under their overcoats, and surrounded the castle. On cue, when the Mayor said his first word, they revealed their message on sticks, pumping vigorously up and down in full view of the cameras. The signs exclaimed the celebration was a travesty against our nation's soldiers. Their exhortation was, "We were a nation at war. To celebrate, as though all is fine, showed disrespect to those risking their lives."

The news media quickly seized the moment. They changed their focus, and turned their attentions to the protesters. News reporters were interviewing any activist who was willing to be on camera. The Mayor, and his cohorts, couldn't get a word in edgewise, partly because someone had disconnected the microphone cord.

As soon as the interviews were finished, and the protesters were sure their voices would be heard, they left the scene for warmer destinations. The night's event aired on the 10PM news that evening, the 7AM news the next morning, and the 6PM news after that. It was also announced that the lighting ceremony had been rescheduled, and there would be heightened security.

## CHAPTER TWENTY-EIGHT

# THE HOT TUB

It was a kickback Sunday afternoon. I sat cross legged on one end of the couch while Debbie sat at the other, with her legs outstretched. We put a pillow under her sprained ankle to keep it elevated, per doctor's orders. It wasn't a severe injury, but she would need to use crutches for a couple of weeks. I had fixed us each a bowl of noodles, peanut butter, and honey toast, and chocolate milk. No complaints from the patient so far. My eyes squinted involuntarily when I looked at Debbie; it helped me focus on just her, the way she used to be, without the distraction of her current unconventional esthetics.

It started snowing around noon, and was expected to continue throughout the day. We had lost reception on our TV, so we turned on the radio to listen to the latest weather update. I didn't want to ruin the chill moment we were having, but I felt it was a good time to ask Debbie how she really felt about Revolution.

"So, do you think he's the one?" I attempted to ask indifferently.

"I'm not sure." she said, appearing open to the conversation. She continued, "I thought at first it was going to work. I'm thinking now, maybe it's moving too fast."

I gave out a sigh of relief, and continue eating.

"Well, don't act so pleased. It's not like he's terrible," Debbie mumbled.

I feared she was about to recant her statement, just to be in opposition. "No, it's cool!" I said, trying to cover up my discontent. We continued to eat, and discuss the past couple of weeks, and started giggling when I imitated the look on Pattie's face when Renekee fell out of the attic.

"What a ditz she is," Debbie said shaking her head. I nodded in agreement, and a drop of water splat into my bowl of noodles.

"What the heck was that? Debbie gasped. Another splat, and we both look up on reflex. Just above my head, a circular part of the ceiling was soaked, and began to form another drip from the little crack in the plaster.

"What the heck is going on up there? Do they have a hot tub or something?" Debbie screeched.

"It's an "or something."

"Meaning?"

"A stock tank."

"What the hell. How do you know this? What's a stock tank!?"

"A place where livestock drink water; I saw Bonita, and Tyrone bringing it in the other night. But that's not the worst of it."

"Oh God, what don't I know? Do I dare ask?"

"Well, funny thing happened when you dozed off in the hospital."

## CHAPTER TWENTY-NINE

# BACK TO REALITY

**B**rian Phillips stood in line at the airport ticket counter. He had had enough of the cold temperatures, and blowing snow that Minnesota had to offer. He longed for his days back at the beach, soaking up the California sun. He'd become thin, and pale since he left home, and hardly recognized himself when he looked in the mirror. He knew it was time to get serious about his life, so he called his Grandma Tweetsie collect, begging for her help. She had always told him, "When you get tired of following your fathers' foolish ideas, you come and live with me."

Brian loved the attention his grandmother gave him. He was her only grandson, and she loved him dearly. Their bond was strong, but Brian had been greatly influenced by his father's lifestyle. Tweetsie was the only mother figure in his life that he could remember. When Brian was growing up he would visit her every weekend at her tiny house on Rotunda Beach. She had a special closet full of the proper clothes for every occasion. There were stylish V-neck sweaters, to be worn with khaki slacks when the ocean air was cool; plaid Bermuda shorts, with polo shirts for more casual outings; speedo swimwear, and Foster Grant sunglasses for when he came of age. Brian would often question his father, asking him why he gave up all the wonderful things Grandma Tweetsie had to offer. Robert's only reply was: "One must search what is best for one's soul son. Someday you may want to take a path of your own, or be content with what I have chosen. The decision is not mine to make." Brian hated when his father would shirk any direct question, and speak in prose.

When he asked about his mother, and where she had been all his life, his father's reply was: "A free spirit cannot be contained." When Brian confronted him on the issue of his future, his father would answer, "Let the eternal light guide you." It concerned Brian there was no plan for college, only the words of his father's wisdom, which were thought of as rhetoric by Grandma Tweetsies' standards.

Robert wasn't always the "free spirit" he seemed to be. He had landed a job right out of college, working as an insurance man for a large corporation. He met Brian's mother, Becky, when she walked into his office one day, applying for a secretarial job. Robert had dreams of having a family, and house with a white picket fence someday. Maybe have two or three kids, and get a dog. Becky's dream was to go to Hollywood, and become a movie star. Robert knew of her aspirations when they first started dating. He was captivated by her beauty, and confident he could change her mind. He took her to the best restaurants, attended the local theatre productions, and bought her beautiful flowers. He even convinced her to go to mass with him on Sunday. Becky enjoyed her time with Robert, it was comfortable. With all his accommodating her every need, she was able to save a lot of money in the hopes to leave for Hollywood soon.

Then it happened. Eight weeks had passed since Becky had given in to Robert's sexual desires, and she now knew her life was never going to be the same. The pregnancy test done at the clinic was positive.

Robert was ecstatic at the news of having a child. He insisted they tell Tweetsie of the pregnancy together, right away. A wedding ceremony took place within two weeks. It was important for the members of the Country Club to meet Becky, before she started to show. Then once the baby arrived it would be stated to as a premature delivery. The plan was made, and there was no turning back.

And so, the blessed event happened. Robert handed out cigars to all his customers. Tweetsie helped Becky find the perfect home with a white picket fence, just like Robert wanted. A little baby boy arrived at eight pounds, four ounces, and they named him Brian, after Roberts great-grandfather. He was so sweet, hardly ever cried. Brian stayed with his grandmother every Sunday morning while Robert, and Becky attended mass. Tweetsie loved to show off her grandson, especially at the Country Club.

"My, what a big baby he is," club members would say. "Oh Yes!" Tweetsie would answer, "so blessed to have him survive his early arrival. We feed him milk, and rice cereal three times a day."

Robert's world was just the way he wanted it. He worked Monday through Friday, leaving eight in the morning, getting home at five every night. He expected dinner on the table promptly at six. He played with Brian for exactly forty-five minutes every night before they ate, and fifteen minutes after, while Becky cleaned up the kitchen. Then it was time for Becky to bathe little Brian, read him a bedtime story, and put him to bed. Robert would watch TV, go to bed, have fifteen minutes of sex, then go to sleep, only to get up the next morning, and start another duplicated day all over again. He was happy. He liked things just the way they were.

When Saturday came, Robert slept until noon. There were no Saturdays to sleep in for Becky, so she dressed little Brian in play clothes, slathered him up with sun screen, and took him to the beach, so as not to wake his father.

One beautiful day at the beach there was a talent scout looking for extras to play in Anette and Frankie's upcoming movie, "Beach Blanket Gone Wild." Becky was bent over, spreading her blanket on the sand. She put little Brian in the middle, and lay down next to him. She wore big, dark sunglasses with a wide brimmed hat. Her legs were long, and tan from their many outings by the ocean. Giving birth to Brian had awarded Becky round, supple, breasts, and they were beautifully displayed in her black and white bikini. She was just what the talent scouts were looking for, and they didn't hesitate to approach her. When they asked if she would be interested in going to Hollywood to do a screen test, her answer, without hesitation, was an immediate "Yes."

Her screen test was so successful it got her a contract for Beach Blanket Gone Wild, Beach Blanket Buddies, and Beach Blanket Under Cover. The studio liked the way she "bounced."

Within a month Robert's life had turned upside down, and he had no choice but to hire a nanny for Brian. Tweetsie said, "Normally I would love to watch him, but, I have my Bridge club on Monday, Yoga on Tuesday, beauty parlor on Wednesdays, riding lessons on Thursday, and lunch with the girls on Friday." Becky would come home on weekends, and she, and Robert would argue. She was too exhausted to do all the domestic things necessary to run a home, and Robert felt he was losing control. The nanny was only paid to watch Brian, and Robert didn't know which end was up anymore. However, the money Becky was earning was hard to pass up. Robert figured their differences would soon dissolve when Hollywood would run out of Beach Blanket movies.

Finally, "Beach Blanket Gone Wild" had come out in theatres. It was Becky's moment, and she and Robert were attending the premier. Becky was in her element, all glitzed up in a beautiful evening gown, hair perfectly coifed, and her eyes dramatically shadowed, and mascaraed. Robert wore a suit and tie, saying it was ridiculous to rent a tux. They sat amongst other bikini girl actresses.

The movie began, and that is when Becky's breasts made their debut. They were gigantic as they bounced across the silver screen. Close up shots of Becky's cleavage took up at least ten feet in size across the movie screen.

Then there were dozens of breasts, bouncing across the movie screen to the tune of bebop music. Becky's figure appeared in a hot pink, polka dot bikini in Technicolor, and made the crowd cheer, and whistle like wolves. There were many sets of boobs, but Becky's were the biggest, and spectacular. Robert was mortified. He lost it, and left the theatre.

After that, Robert never recovered. He no longer wanted the house, fence, or dog. He quit his job, and spent his days with his son. After Becky filed for divorce, he sold his house, and rented a small bungalow by the beach. He invested in a hot dog stand on the boardwalk, so Brian would be able to be with him all day until he became of school age. During the time Brian was in school, Robert joined the "International Society of Krishna's Consciousness," donned a Saffron robe, and spent his afternoons at the airports drifting, and chanting mantras to his new-found Hindu god. He became celibate, and had no desire to continue the life he once had.

When it was Brian's turn at the airline counter, he picked up the ticket his grandmother had arranged for him. Boarding the plane to Los Angeles he took a seat next to the window, trying to remain as low-key as possible. He felt uncomfortable in his outfit; the wing tipped shoes were a half size too big, the black slacks he was wearing barely reached his ankles, and the button-down color on his white shirt needed a good washing. He stared out the window watching the men in blue jumpsuits busily tend to their various duties, loading luggage on the plane, and filling it with fuel. A young lady took the seat next to him, and quickly clipped her seat belt.

"Is this your first flight?" she asked animatedly.

"Not exactly," Brian replied shyly.

"Oh, this is mine. I've never been to California either. First time." She giggled, "I guess we get to eat on the plane too! I wonder what we're having? I hope it's good. I was so nervous this morning I couldn't dream of having a bowl of cereal. I'm Tammy by the way." She held out her hand for a friendly shake. Her bubbly behavior matched her caricature appearance. Brian began to relax, and smiled; taking her hand he says, "Nice to meet you, my name's Brian, but my friends call me Ambrosia."

Sitting on the corner of 6th and Market was a man wearing a fake beard, a sheet over his winter coat, and high-top tennis shoes. While pan handling, he burned incense in a little cast iron mettle pot, and sang, "haree, haree krseeehna" as suggested by a most unusual acquaintance. His feet were cold, and he wished he hadn't given up his wing tipped shoes. Maybe the day's pan handling would give him enough for a pair of boots from the Army surplus.

## CHAPTER THIRTY

# ALL AFLOAT

Mrs. Odettes distant cousin, Sully, owned a small gas station close to downtown St. Paul. With a large garage, it had enough space for two vehicles, allowing Sully to do oil changes, and tune ups. He offered one of the spaces to the Daughters of Norway, to work on their float. A small store, barely big enough to have more than three people in it at a time, was attached to the garage, that also doubled as his office. A glass case was stocked full of candy bars, and its Formica counter top barely had enough room for an old cash register, a receipt book, and an old, washed out bean can full of pens with greasy finger prints. There were three doors: the front entrance, with a picture window next to it that had a large decal of a red, and yellow bottle of antifreeze; the door behind the counter that entered into the smallest and most disgusting toilet in the world with a filthy, rusty, sink, and a mirror on a medicine cabinet holding one bottle of mercurochrome; and a door that went from the office into the garage area; a single chrome stool with black, worn out, torn vinyl mended with tape on the seat sits at the counter, and a silver, and glass cigarette machine butted up against the only wall without a door. On it read a sign "must be 18." An old radio was placed on top of the machine, and the dial was set on WCCO, with another sign reading "do not touch."

Every day after work the Unit Control Department worked diligently helping Mrs. Odettes, and The Daughters of Norway create, what they hoped would be, the winning float of the "Winter Carnival Torchlight Parade." The Daughters' vision was to build a small fishing village, simulating their homeland. Our department thought it was a stretch of the imagination, but everyone gave it their all.

Through Sully's connections, we had a forty-foot flatbed trailer to work our magic on. He had volunteered to pull the trailer in the parade with his 1967 Pontiac GTO convertible muscle car. Mrs. Odettes asked her cousin if he was sure his car would have enough power to pull the heavy flatbed. He assured her not to worry; his 4-link rear suspension could pull TWO flatbeds that size if it had to.

On the night of the parade the top of the convertible would be put down, and a blue velvet blanket will lay over it. The visiting King and Queen of Norway would sit on the blanket, and wave to the crowd, with the comfort of the car heater running full blast for warmth. Mrs. Odette's, being this year's chairperson, would have the privilege of riding in the front seat. Sully, of course, would drive the car.

We started decorating in the middle of the flatbed, creating an oval shape lake by using silver, and blue spray paint on the wood floor. Papier Mache' was used to form a slight berm to resemble snow that had been cleared from the ice. We painted it with glue, and sprinkled it with Ivory Snowflakes detergent mixed with glitter; a concoction Patty remembered from grade school. With the remaining mixture, we gave a light dusting on the lake. At the front of the flatbed, on one side of the lake, we constructed a small fishing shanty made of heavy corrugated cardboard, which was painted brown with streaks of black to make it look like weathered lumber. A wooden bench was placed on the imaginary ice, in front of the shanty. This would be the staging for one of The Daughters of Norway, who would be wearing an old fisherman's costume, pretending to be ice fishing.

On the other side of the painted lake was a five-foot by five-foot cottage built of balsam wood. A window was cut out on each side, facing the sidewalks of many spectators the Torchlight was known to have. An electrician donated his time, and helped wire the Christmas lights throughout the float. Microphones were placed on hooks next to the windows in the cottage, and two speakers were placed back to back on its roof. Two of The Daughters of Norway were to dress in traditional folk costumes of elaborate embroidery, bright red shawls, and bonnets of indigo blue fabric. They were also members of the church choir, and would sing the songs of Norway to the crowd as they waved looking out the windows. The electrical cord was cleverly hidden under the berm, and connecting to a small generator that was placed in the ice shanty.

We swaged crepe paper streamers of red, indigo blue, and white around the edges of the float to represent the flag of Norway, and we were finished. It was well thought out, and looked fantastic. Everyone applauded, and complimented Mrs. Odettes for her determination, instruction, and attention to detail.

## CHAPTER THIRTY-ONE

# AT THE FLAT

**D**espite our unconventional decor, things at the flat almost seemed back to normal. I made Debbie and myself each a cup of Swiss Miss, and we chilled on our sofa; having moved it to the other side of the living room. A bucket, on loan from the caretaker, sat under the ceiling leak, and was half full of water. Every few seconds a drip would form in our ceiling, and plop into its target below.

Debbie's temporary dependency on crutches proved to be an inconvenience for Revolution, and he suggested they wait until she recovered before resuming their relationship.

"You mean he's dumping you because of your foot?" I asked, with obvious displeasure of his existence in my tone.

"It's not my foot, it's my ankle. And he's not dumping me; we're on a break until I can be more mobile."

"Sounds bogus."

"You really hate him, don't you?"

"I don't "hate" him, I just don't "trust" him. I think your karma radar has been on the blink ever since the two of you met."

"Maybe you're right." Debbie agreed, "I've been thinking about Renekee more, and more. When he showed up at the hospital with flowers I felt he really cared. I couldn't believe it. Revolution doesn't believe in giving flowers; he says it's stripping the earth of its beauty."

"Then why do they call themselves flower children?"

"I'm not sure they are. I know the names are flowery, but there seems to be an unspoken edge."

She continued on about Renekee. How caring, and concerned he was. How he always made her laugh. There was very little laughter with Revolution.

"Believe me. He's your knight." I winked, and smiled my approval. "Maybe he realized what he had lost, and now deserves a second chance." I have no idea why I'm giving her advice; I know nothing about relationships, seeing how I've never had one.

A knock on the door put a hold on our conversation. I padded over to look out through the peep hole.

"Shit!" I whispered, "Its Tyrone."

"Let me handle this," Debbie said as she crutched her way into action. She approached the door, but stopped far enough back allowing for clearance. As I open to let Tyrone enter, I took my place at her side, for spectator purposes only.

"Bonita says you got a leak?" Tyrone said. He stood aggressively, taking up our entire doorway, pulled a comb out of his back pocket, and started grooming his Elvis locks. His pretense wasn't fooling anyone.

"Really, that's what she called it?" Debbie's animosity toward Bonita rang loud, and clear. We stepped aside, and a plethora of after shave consumed our space as he passed us. Falling into line, we followed him to the area in question. He looked at the ceiling, and we looked at him. His "Mom" tattoo now gave new meaning to the word nuts. I held back a snicker, and glanced at Debbie who was watching him closely. The box of cigarettes tucked under the sleeve of his T-shirt showed he had changed his brand, and his biceps appeared to have added an additional bulge.

"So, what do you suppose is causing this?" Debbie asked with an accusatory tone.

"Maybe a leak in the piping," he said.

"In the middle of the living room where there is no piping?" I asked. I didn't know much about plumbing, but I did know most of the pipes are either in the kitchen or bathroom.

"I think we heard some splashing noises the other day, didn't we Mia," Debbie said without looking in my direction. Her stare was focused on Tyrone.

"What happened to your foot?" Tyrone asked.

"It's my ankle. None of your business" she answered.

He moved the bucket, and stood directly below the cracked plaster to get a better look. Tilting his head back, he looked up at the ceiling for only a second, when another drip fell, hitting him right between the eyes. That was when I noticed the leech on the back of his neck.

## CHAPTER THIRTY-TWO

# FOOL ME ONCE, SHAME ON YOU. FOOL ME TWICE...

It had been five days since the skating incident, and Debbie's sprain was on the mend. She had mastered the skill of crutch walking, and was feeling up to getting out of the flat. We decided to attend the rescheduled lighting celebration together. The temperature was supposed to drop to three below zero, so warmth took precedence over fashion. I noticed Debbie wasn't wearing her beaded headband, and her old hair style was starting to take hold. We both wore jeans, and sweaters. She pulled her ski jacket out of the closet, and handed me mine, then asked if I would help her with her boots. I knelt down to slip one on.

"Hey Saffron, aren't you wearing your clogs tonight?" I said, staring down at the boot. I tried not to laugh, but I couldn't stop myself.

"Do you want to live to see tomorrow? Say you're sorry," she snapped.

"But love means never having to say you're sorry," I replied; tongue in cheek.

"Very funny." She smirked while grinding a noogie onto my head.

We took the 17 downtown, and transferred onto a direct express bus to the castle. Tonight's crowd was much larger, due to the publicity from the first lighting. The city's Mayor, and other dignitaries, once again gathered on the small stage in front of the castle, and the local news teams are summoned one more time to attend. Police cars parked strategically around the area, but the officers remained in their warm, cozy spaces; a kiosk of coffee, and hot cocoa had secured a spot close to the podium; the State Fair Tom Thumb Donut Wagon came out of hibernation for the event, sending out an aroma reminiscent of summer days; a woman selling woolen nose warmers for fifty cents gave many of the spectators a beak-like appearance; a couple of mimes in various layers of black, and white were annoying everyone, and anyone they encountered with their silent mimicry, and juggling of snowballs, and a left-over group of holiday carolers were trying out their new repertoire of Frank Sinatra tunes. The exploitation by the media of the first lighting had made the second lighting open season for any enthusiast in the city.

Without delay, the Mayor spoke into the microphone. "Welcome," he said. He held in his left hand the extension cord connected to the lights, and in the other hand he held the cord for the power source. Once he realized he was on camera, he broke into smile, and began talking about his upcoming election. With an aggressive nudge from his secretary, he was urged to stick to the subject at hand. "Plug in the damn lights" his very cold assistant whispered from behind him. At the Mayors expense, her voice was picked up by the microphone, and the crowd chuckled.

"Without further ado," he continued with embarrassment, "let the festivities of our Winter Carnival officially begin." He connected the cords, and a strobe of rainbow colors instantly panned the castle made of ice; making the fantasy come to life. The freezing crowd clapped, but the sound was muted with the thud of slapping mittens. The mimes were mouthing annoying gestures of ooohs, and aaaaahs while holding their arms in the air, as if they were under arrest. Small children were yelling "look, look," and "I'm hungry, I want a donut." Everyone had forgotten how cold it was for a brief second, taking in the beauty of a fantasy come to life… until a loud boom drew the crowds' attention toward the center of the structure.

"Wow, I didn't know there were going to be fireworks," I exclaimed as we all stood in disbelief. Ice, and snow started shooting straight up from the middle of the castle, and a second boom made the horns of the unicorns fall to the ground.

"Those aren't fireworks!" Debbie shouted, "Someone's blowing up the ice!"

Once the mayor realized what was happening he jumped off the podium and hid behind a tree. His secretary took the microphone, and announced to clear the area. The squad cars turned on their sirens, and their rooftop cherries began flashing red strobes across the area. The police, now bounding out of their cars, were randomly scurrying without a plan, and tried to catch anyone who looked suspicious. The mimes had broken their code of silence, and screamed at 80 decibels as they ran for shelter. Mothers grabbed their children by the arms, shuffling as quickly as possible across the frozen ground to safety. Tom Thumb closed its window, not to be opened again until August for the Great Minnesota Get Together.

Debbie was moving at a snail's pace, with her crutches, over the slippery ground. I hunched like a Quasimodo working defense, trying to keep the frenzied crowd from trampling her. The castle lights started flickering, and on impulse I turned to look back. Three people were about to set off another bomb under the draw-bridge to the castle. At first, I didn't recognize Cosmic River, and Hyacinth, but Revolution's Army attire was unmistakable.

"Debbie look!" I shouted. She turned around, and without hesitation, broke into an expedient hobble toward Revolution. When she got within striking distance she blurted, "You Son of a Bitch!" The look on his face was priceless, as he impulsively turned toward her at the sound of her voice. She dropped one crutch, and flipped the other so that she was holding the narrow end. Her baton twirling lessons had finally paid off. With one fell swoop she slugged Revolution upside the head to home-run proportions.

Falling back from the force landed Debbie flat on her back. Revolution spun like a top, landing face first in the snow. He lost consciousness long enough for Debbie to recover from her fall, and slither over the frozen ground. Climbing onto Revolution's back, she took position right between his shoulder blades. He began moaning as he started coming to.

Cosmic River, and Hyacinth spontaneously broke into a sprint, intending to leave their Charlie Manson protégé behind. I picked up the discarded crutch, and whipped it like a boomerang, catching Hyacinth behind the knees, making her topple into Cosmic River, where they both landed in a heap. By this time the police were on the scene with cuffs in hand.

"There should be one more," Debbie said to the police.

"Yeah, he's kinda pale, and wears a sheet," I add.

"He's not here." Revolution mumbled as he came to, "He went back to California."

Cosmic River, Hyacinth, and Revolution were each thrown into individual squad cars. A fourth car was offered to us for an escort home.

On our ride back to the flat I knew Debbie would be weary. I remained silent until she asked, "Mia, on the night you were put in the lineup, what did you say everyone was wearing?"

"T-shirt, flannel shirt, and a ball cap. Why?"

"So was Revolution. He left them in the laundry room that night, telling me they were too wet from the rain to wear."

We rode the rest of the way home in silence.

## CHAPTER THIRTY-THREE

# ICE FISHING

I ce Fishing: Verb, Gerund or present participle: fishing through holes in ice on a lake or river.

If you live in the North, and get a little stir crazy in the winter months, you ice fish.

Ice fishing is like yoga: To sit in front of a hole in the ice, typically in subzero temperatures, unable to do anything but stare at your line, gives one time to reflect, contemplate and dream.

Ice fishing takes skill: When winter temperatures freeze the top of the water, and snow covers it by a foot or two, the fish have no other choice than to swim as close as they can to the bottom for food, and oxygen. There are fewer minnows for the larger species to feast upon, so when a hook dangles a tidbit in front of them, they are sure to bite. The key is to guess how far down to drop a line, and hope you chose an area where the fish might be.

Ice fishing ain't for sissies: To dress for ice fishing is to use every article of clothing you can possibly cover yourself with. Dressing in layers is the key to staying warm. Cover that with a sealed, insulated dry suit, heavy chopper mittens, a lamb's skin hat with ear flaps, scarf, box of snuff in one pocket, and a fifth of schnapps in the other. January temperatures are usually in the single digits above zero when the sun shines, and below zero when night falls. If it starts blowing, it can reach wind chills as cold as thirty-five degrees below zero.

Ice fishing has important equipment: A small rod, stick, or fishing pole holds a fishing line with brightly colored jigs, or lures of bait, typically wax worms. The angler holds the choice of gear over the hole, and drops the line in, letting the bait drop to the estimated depth to attract a fish. The angler then lifts the pole, giving it a jiggle. Often times you just need a bucket to sit on, and then carry the fish home, but if you are a serious angler you may want to invest in an ice house, or shanty as some prefer to call them. This is a structure usually made of plywood, and is approximately seven feet by seven feet in size, and tall enough to stand in. It has to have enough room for a gas space heater, and two lawn chairs for comfort, as well as a tackle box or two. The floor has a large opening that is situated over the hole in the ice, and a small smoke stack on the roof for ventilation.

Ice fishing is dangerous: When the temperatures drop, and the ice freezes even more, it expands; causing it to buckle, and heave, creating pressure ridges, and open ice. Even four feet of ice can crack apart; when it starts you hear a loud shocking snap, almost like thunder, and lightning combined into one. You can feel movement, but aren't sure which way to run, and then you see the crack, and hope you made the right decision. There's no time for second guessing, and traveling on foot is the most rational means of passage. When the sound has subsided, you look to see if the lake has swallowed either your pickup, ice house, or both.

Ice fishing allows for an off sense of humor: To gather with friends on a frozen lake, is to know the humor of an Ole and Lena joke. The cast of fictional characters are usually Ole, Lena his wife, and Sven, Ole's friend, whose personalities were created over the years by the misinterpretation of the English language. The short stories, and jokes are typically spoken with broken accents resembling the Nordic countries.

Example: When Ole and Sven get together it's usually their stupidity that becomes the joke.

Example: Ole and Sven go to a funeral. Ole says to Sven, "Remind me again who died." Sven says, "I tink it's dat guy over dare in the casket."

<u>Ice fishing has a silent oath</u>: Never divulge your best fishing spot, and never admit "it's too cold to fish."

## CHAPTER THIRTY-FOUR

# TOURNAMENT DAY

Forest Lake was known as the bass capitol of Minnesota, and was the location of one of the largest fishing tournaments in the state. Its lakes were named First Lake, Second Lake, and Third Lake; connected by wide waterways, making it perfect fishing with a high fish population of Northern Pike, Large-mouth Bass, Walleye, and many pan fish. The small town would easily draw more than four thousand competitors to its contest, and added to that, vendors to feed the anglers; spectators to watch and socialize; local, and city news reporters taking pictures, and writing the facts. With a potential to double in size, if the weather was above zero, it could possibly triple.

The day before the tournament, a fifteen-acre circle was cleared, and roped off on First Lake. A large group of men worked the early hours of the morning, before the event, drilling over eight thousand ten inch holes in the clearing, marking each one with a red flag. Another ten acres would be cleared for parking vehicles, a shuttle drop off, and food vendors.

Registration started at 7AM, and the tournament commenced at 10AM. You had to be at least 16 years old to compete, but children under 16 were allowed to fish, as long as they are accompanied by an adult. Each contestant would fish from one hole only. The winnings were various sporting goods equipment, and a large cash prize for the biggest fish (which entices many amateurs). Anyone was allowed to drop a line through a hole in the ice, as long as he had a fishing license, and was registered.

Once registered contestants waited, usually holding a five-gallon plastic bucket filled with a jigging stick, extra fishing line, and bait. Once the town siren blew, it was no holds barred. You ran, or shuffled (depending on how slick the ice might be), to find your fishing hole as quickly as possible, bait the hook; drop the line in the water; flipped the bucket, and took a seat. Waiting could take all the patience of a saint, but it was important to keep your eye on the prize, as they say.

Once you caught a fish it was imperative to get it over to the judges, without losing precious time, to record the species, weight, and length. The fish was tagged, and kept in a stock tank. You returned to your spot as quickly as possible, in hopes of catching another fish, only bigger. When the contest was finished the winners were announced, prizes were awarded, and pictures were taken of the winning fish and its angler. Then all fish were released back into the lake.

Keeping the contenders honest was serious business. Jerry Larson, from the little town of Holyoke, worked the registration table, along with a couple of appointed deputies, and the Forest Lake Sheriff. Jerry may have been gentle as a kitten, but his lumberjack build had been known to intimidate anyone who broke the rules. He knew everything about fishing, and a little bit about crooks. It had only been a year ago that he had worked with the Minneapolis police, providing information for a suspicious case of fraud involving a phony church supper in Holyoke, and counterfeit raffle tickets sold by two women from Minneapolis.

Jerry never went anywhere without his wife, Judy, who tended a concession stand next to the registration table. Dressed in her mouton fur hooded parka, and fur laced boots, brought out her North Indian heritage. She handed out free coffee to the contestants, and sold Jerry's homemade cookies for a nominal price, raising money for the Department of Natural

Resources. Her strong resemblance of an Eskimo, and her infectious laughter, often intrigued customers to congregate around her stand, warming their hands holding the hot drinks, and listening to Judy tell of her ancestry. She had, what Jerry called, a gift. "She's my better half," he often said. Her keen perception of honesty was as simple as looking into one's eyes. If the winning fish was of a doubtful nature, meaning caught elsewhere, and smuggled in, Judy would take a good look at the contender and call it as she saw it. She didn't need a lie detector to determine if the winner was speaking the truth, but for the satisfaction of the tournament board, they had been known to resort to the mechanical intelligence. Judy was always spot on.

CHAPTER THIRTY-FIVE

# RECONNECTING

**R**evolution's departure from Debbie's life couldn't have happened at a better time had she planned it. She decided to skip the fishing tournament, and stayed at the flat, allowing her ankle to heal. Renekee had called, and plans were made for him to hang out while she convalesced. I, on the other hand, had dreams of catching the big one. I had been fishing the Forest Lake fishing tournament since I was ten years old. This year's plan was to meet up with my childhood friend, Goldie. We hadn't seen each other since graduation; she had gone off to college, and I got a job in the city.

Saturday morning Finbar picked me up at 5AM, and we drove to Forest Lake. He dropped me off at home, and I grabbed a quick breakfast with my parents, filling them in on the latest antics of the past week. Their mouths are agape by the time I took my last bite of toast. I changed into my dad's long johns, a sweater, blue jeans, wool socks, insulated overalls, and mutton chops. My mom had knit me a ski mask, and scarf for Christmas, which I had conveniently forgotten to bring back to my flat. It now sat on a table by the door, waiting for my return. I felt an obligation to wear them to the event, and I figured I could use the extra warmth. Sunshine yellow wouldn't have been my choice of color, but I knew Mom was proud of her creation, and excited for me to show it off. Luckily my old snow boots still fit me. I cringed when I saw my dad's clodhoppers, (as my mother called them) sitting by the door for me as a backup. I remarked to my parents that I looked like the local Yeti under cover. They both laughed, and my dad said, as he patted me on the shoulder, "Keep your eye on the prize, and don't fish like your grandpa."

My grandpa was known to be one of the best fishermen in the area. You could find him at the lake on any given winter day by daybreak. Usually he had fished for Crappies, just enough for dinner that day. If fishing was good, and he caught extra, he would clean, and filet them; bringing them into town to give to Gladys, to cook for the residents at the nursing home. She would put them in the freezer, and when she finally had enough for everyone at the home, they'd have a fish fry.

Well, one-day Grandpa was at Lake Henry fishing. He heard the sound of a vehicle coming down the road to the lake, but he didn't dare turn, and take a "look see" as to who it was for fear he would miss a nibble. It was his good friend Donny puttering along in his rusted-out Ford pickup. He slowly came to a stop, and parked next to Grandpa's red Datsun pickup. Donny left his truck running, for fear in the sub-zero temperature it may not start up again. He just never knew when his clunker was going to give up for good, and he didn't want to be stuck out in the middle of nowhere on a cold winters day. Donny was always prepared to fish at any given moment, dressed in insulated coveralls, clunky boots, and leather WWII Pilot hat with ear flaps. He hopped out of his truck, and hiked out to where Grandpa sat on his bucket, staring at the hole in the ice.

"How they bitin?" Donny asked quietly so as not to scare the fish.

"They ain't" Grandpa mumbled.

"I bet Gladys has a pot of coffee brewing," Donny said. "How bout we take a run into town".

Well, it was eight below with a wind chill of minus twenty-two, Grandpa was getting cold, and a cup of hot coffee sounded pretty good. He flipped his plastic bucket; put his stick, and jigger inside, and the two of them hopped in Donny's car, leaving for town.

Now time got away from the fishermen, one story leading to another. Gladys kept pouring the coffee as the two men kibitzed with the residents, swapping tall tales of the one that got away. But when the sirens started blaring in town, and a commotion of cars went rumbling past the nursing home, Donny and Grandpa got curious.

"Holy smokes! What's going on?" Grandpa asked Gladys.

"I just got a call from Louise at the Texaco, somebody has gone through the ice at Lake Henry," she said.

"By golly, we better get a move-on Donny. They might need our help!" Grandpa said, and he and Donny quickly hopped in Donny's pickup, and followed the stream of cars headed to Lake Henry.

They both became more than concerned, when they saw all the cars were headed to Grandpa's fishing spot. As they drove down the narrow, icy path, several cars had already spun out, and landed in the two foot of snow that had drifted alongside by the ditch. The two men continued puttering along in Donny's pickup, until they got next to Grandpa's pickup, of which there was parked an ambulance, fire truck, and Doc. Bendickson's car.

Grandpa, and Donny looked out at the lake. Since they had left for coffee the ice had buckled and a large hole had opened right next to Grandpa's fishing bucket. They looked at each other, and knew what someone had misconstrued. The two men approached the group of rescuers that were huddled, discussing strategies.

"What seems to be the problem?" Grandpa asked the Sheriff.

"We think old man..." the Sheriff turned to look at who asked the question, and stopped talking when he saw the apparition before him.

"Who you calling an old man?" Grandpa smiled.

I borrowed my dad's 65 Ford pickup truck; it was a little rusty, and had seen better days, but still ran like a top. I drove to pick up Goldie, honking the horn as I pulled in her driveway. She came bopping out her front door with her fishing stick, and bucket in hand. She was slightly shorter than me, had cool blue eyes, and a smirk ready to break into a smile at any second. She had a keen eye for mischief, and at times our communication relied strictly on facial expressions.

"Nice outfit," I commented.

Goldie was dressed in a white snowmobile suit with red piping accents, cinched in at her tiny waist with a red belt, white insulated gloves, black boots, and a blue stocking cap with matching scarf, completing the ensemble.

"Oh thanks! I got it for Christmas. Do you really like it?"

"You look like Evil Knievel's little sister."

"And you look like Earnest Hemmingway under-cover."

"Point taken." We never took each other too seriously.

"So, what's our plan?" Goldie asked.

"First stop, Arnie's Bait Shop. We'll get our fishing license, and bait; then head over to the lake for registration."

"Roger," she replied.

We listened to WCCO on the radio as we drove to Arnie's bait shop. It was the only possible station to get tuned into on the old pick-up radio. I don't think it has budged from 8-3-0 on the dial since my dad drove it off the sales lot. I figured the little needle was rusted in place. The nice thing about listening to WCCO is that you will get the current weather conditions, and forecast about every ten minutes. The bad thing about listening to WCCO is that you will get the current weather conditions, and forecast about every ten minutes. The current condition, as of five minutes ago, was eight above, and the forecast was for a high of 15 degrees above zero. Not exactly a heat wave but it could be worse.

We arrived at the little brown painted building with the name "Arnies" burned into a slice of pine wood, hanging above the entrance. It sat about fifty yards back from the shoreline of First Lake, and its large picture window had a scenic view of what you may see on a Christmas card. Arnie carried every type of tackle known to man; tanks full of minnows waiting for their death, and barrels of dirt housing night crawlers the size of small snakes. The place was packed with out-of-towners hoping to catch the "Big One." As Goldie, and I entered the shop we were concerned we wouldn't get the bait we wanted. I liked fishing with night crawlers; Goldie was a minnow fan.

Arnie knew us well, "since we were tadpoles" he would say. He was a sweet old guy around his mid-seventies, and had worked in the bait shop his whole life. As a kid he helped his dad, Arnie Senior, run the shop until the old man died at the age of 94. The name of the bait shop stayed the same, but patrons continued to call Arnie, "Junior." Arnie Junior had one son, and named him Arnie, who in turn would be called "Little Arnie." Little Arnie grew up, went to college, and became a doctor, working at the Forest Lake clinic. The old timers in town still called him "little Arnie.… the doctor." Everyone in town figured when Arnie Junior died the bait shop would too.

A bell was hooked to the top of the door, alerting Arnie every time someone entered, or exited his store. As Goldie and I entered, the bell jingled, and the old man looked over, and gave us a smile. Little Arnie the doctor was helping his dad out during the big event, taking care of customers behind the counter. "It's about time you two tadpoles showed up," Arnie Junior said in a loud voice with undertones of laughter. "I got your stuff over here," he said, waving for us to come forward. Arnie Junior had set aside a box of black dirt, and twenty night-crawlers for me. Goldie got a plastic container of twenty minnows. Arnie Junior would only accept payment for our licenses'. "Go catch the big one" he ordered as we shuffled our way out the door.

We hustled over to the shuttle, and caught a ride out to the contest area. The registration line was long, with about 30 people ahead of us. We quickly took our place.

"Hey, look up ahead," Goldie said, "isn't that Kerry Anne?"

"Looks like it," I answer; perusing the line ahead of us.

Kerry Anne was a former classmate. Like most of our classmates, we started out in kindergarten together, and through the duration of twelve years of school, learned about life collectively along the way. Back in those days of kindergarten we knew very little about procreation. Our parents did whatever they could to avoid the subject of where babies came from. The word pregnant was never used, but sometimes we could overhear adults whispering the letters P G. The word divorce was always used in combination with the phrase "run-around." Adults treated the "situation" of pregnancy as something enigmatic, and should be whispered about. But, when the same women who was whispered about, for having been known to have done the much-discussed reference to sex, gave birth she became admired and praised. The blessed event was now big news. But the question of how "it" escaped the abdomen was left to our five-year-old imaginations. This was another uncomfortable conundrum for our parents to explain. After long discussions in the cloakroom, in elementary school, it was unanimous the infant escaped through the belly button.

Even in kindergarten, we took pleasure in repeating rumors over-heard in our homes. Whenever adults lowered their voices to a hush, every child in the universe knew it was time to raise their antenna. On a daily basis, some student would have overheard gossip, and innuendo to share at recess. One time on the playground by the monkey bars, a rumor had started about what was thought to be Kerry Anne's true identity. The basis of the rumor was her strong affinity for Howdy Doody. Not only did Kerry Anne have bright red hair, and freckles, she also had a Howdy Doody doll, cow girl boots, plaid shirt, and a vest. We all envied her simulation of the TV icon, until the day the rumor started. Trixie Goldman said that Karrie Anne's mother ran-around with Howdy. Trixie's dad was a lawyer, and Trixie was known for her extravagant imagination, and large vocab-ulary. Now common sense tells us this wasn't possible. Howdy was made of wood. But at the time it made perfect sense when Trixie said, "Through divine intervention, you could have a wooden baby. Take, for instance, the case of Pinocchio versus Geppetto, my dad said it was a real story, and then Disney made a cartoon out of it."

Goldie and I didn't believe a word Trixie said then, nor now. We ratted her out to our teacher Mrs. Hanson, who had the whole class stand by their desks, put their hand on their hearts, and pledge to the flag not to talk about others on the playground, or in the cloakroom anymore.

We got Kerry Anne's attention by flailing our arms, and yelling. She turned in response to our commotion, and waves. "I'll see you after you register," she yelled back to us. We gave her a thumbs up.

The temperature had now climbed to a balmy eighteen degrees above zero. WCCO was only off by three degrees. The line was building behind us, and everyone did what they could to stay warm; stomping feet, and slapping arms together. I even surrendered to pulling the ski mask over my face, regardless of how silly I felt. We were only two people away from the registration table when Judy Larson took a cup of coffee, and a handful of Jerrys' cookies to a couple in line several people behind us. Her boots crunched, and squeaked on the ice as she walked passed us, with the steam of the coffee trailing behind, wafting our senses. I could hear Judy say to the women, "My goodness, you must be a dedicated wife to accompany your husband on this cold winters day in your condition!" I turned to see what she is talking about, as Judy handed the coffee, and cookies to a very pregnant Bonita. Tyrone was standing next to her, gushing like a proud father to be, but Judy's smile turned solemn when her eyes met Bonita's.

I froze at the sight, then Goldie gave me a nudge, "Snap out of it, it's our turn to register."

## CHAPTER THIRTY-SIX

# SOMETHING FISHY

**W**e signed in, and ran over to where Kerry Anne stood waiting patiently for the town siren to blow. I fill my friends in on the questionable condition of the pregnant lady, and the stock tank the couple kept in their apartment, above mine. It was pretty clear to us what their plan was, and we agreed we were the only ones able to sabotage it.

We had no time to waste, and needed to devise a plan as quickly as possible. Together, we decided Goldie would be the one to distract Tyrone, while Kerry Anne created a diversion by approaching Bonita with questions about her pregnancy. Neither Bonita nor Tyrone had recognized me in my ski mask so far, but I didn't want to take the chance of either of them hearing my voice, although I'm not so sure I could give them that much credit. They may be skillful at being dishonest, but I don't consider them to be the sharpest knives in the drawer. It was decided I would be the one to inform registration of the facts, as I knew them. It was now only five minutes until starting. We quickly reviewed our plan; we couldn't afford any mistakes.

The siren blew and the anglers began their race to, what they hoped, was their prize fishing hole. It was pandemonium, and impossible for anyone to be concerned with someone following them. We strategically secured our fishing holes only twenty feet away from Tyron's. We took our calculated positions, and with synchronized accuracy, flipped our buckets and drop our lines. With the stage set, it was now time to start the show. Goldie had a straight view from Tyrone's fishing hole; she waited for him to get in position, dropping his line.

Clearly Tyrone was anxiously looking about the area, rather than at the hole in the ice waiting for a bite. Goldie began her performance; Act I, she took off her stocking cap and tousles her hair. Kerry Anne and I discreetly watched; we're impressed at her moves. Tyrone was instantaneously captivated, as we had suspected he would be. Goldie tried to apply a fresh glob of pot'o'gloss to her lips, seductively, but it was frozen solid. Like a true actress, she didn't let that problem interfere with her performance.

Kerry Anne was more excited about apprehending a criminal, than catching a fish, and forgot to bait her hook. She dropped her line in the hole.

"You're never gonna catch a fish without bait," I said to her.

"Who cares," she giggled. "We've got a much bigger fish to catch."

"Ok," I whispered, "are we ready for action?"

"Does a bear shit in the woods?" my cohorts responded in unison. It was good to be home.

Tyrone was making himself look busy, playing with his tackle and fiddling around with a leech. Bonita was rummaging through her tapestry bag, most likely for a snack. Goldie made her move over to Tyrone's spot.

"Well... hello," she was seductive to Jane Mansfield proportions, and might have overplayed her part a tiny bit. She struck a pose; Kerry Anne and I were stymied.

"Did she just throw her head back and laugh?" Kerry Anne asked, as we both took pause and marveled at Goldie's transition.

"Maybe it's the inside Goldie coming out… But whatever, you're on Kerry," I directed. She followed her cue, and without missing a beat got into character. Like a phantom she appeared at Bonita's side, who was still digging through her bag.

Kerry Anne spoke: "Watcha looking for?"

"None of your business," Bonita snapped without looking up.

"When's your baby due?" Kerry Anne continued, "Is this your first one? I suppose you want a boy. Everyone wants a boy the first time. I think it's a guy thing."

"Who's askin?" She looked at Kerry Anne annoyingly.

"Me, didn't you see my lips move?" Kerry Anne wasn't backing down. In the meantime, Goldie had succeeded in getting Tyrone's attention.

"Do I know you?" Tyrone asked, looking bewildered, interested, and horny. Something about her seemed very familiar to him. Once again Goldie threw her head back making her locks of blonde hair bounce in the frigid air.

"Do you want to know me?" Goldie asked in her best breathy voice. She smiled and continued, "Names Goldie…Goldie Knievel. Maybe you know my brother."

At this moment Tyrone had lost all composure. He had been a huge fan of Evil Knievel, following Evil's every stunt, saving every newspaper clipping and magazine article. He had cut them out, and taped them to his cell wall, back when he was doing time in Stillwater prison. To meet Evils sister would be an act of God, a sign. He, like his mother, would praise the Lord when suitable.

"Something seems to be wrong with my fishing stick, and my line is all tangled. Could you help me?" Goldie whimpered while giving Tyrone her best bedroom eyes approach.

Tyrone's excitement began to rise, and his masculine cravings were climbing the testosterone thermometer. "No harm in helping Evil's sister," he said smiling. He stopped what he was doing, and without a second thought of Bonita, followed Goldie back to her fishing spot like a bloodhound hot on the trail.

Now that Goldie and Kerry Anne were in position, I scooted as fast as I could across the ice to the registration table, and started telling my story. Jerry and the Sheriff listened to my tale absorbedly. There was no Tyrone on the roster, as the men and I looked over the entries, but there was a Christopher Alby!

"That's him!" I yelled. Jerry and the sheriff look at each other, and then turn their attention across the circle where the party in question had selected to fish. At that very moment Kerrie Anne had lost her tolerance for Bonita's belligerence.

"So, when did you say your baby is due?" Kerry Anne asked Bonita once more.

"I didn't. Don't you need to bait a hook pip squeak?" Bonita was irritated, and her usual rude self.

"Who you calling pip squeak?"

"You, short stack." Bonita feared Tyrone's distraction was going to interfere with their plan, and she was losing her patience dealing with the little red head in her face. She needed to get rid of Kerry Anne pronto, and retrieve Tyrone as quickly as possible.

"I don't think I like you," Kerrie Anne declared. This conversation wasn't in the rehearsed dialogue, but she felt Bonita's insults had gone too far.

"Too bad. Now go away before I swat you like a bug," Bonita bullied.

Kerrie Anne might be small, but she didn't take guff from anybody. The pregnant woman's aggressive behavior didn't scare Kerrie Anne one bit, and she impulsively gave Bonita a shove. It was so spur-of-the-moment that Kerrie Anne didn't realize the force behind it. Bonita was totally taken off guard, and began slipping with a backward shuffle, then a forward shuffle, and then another backward shuffle, ending with a splat as her ass hit the ice. A clear liquid gushed out from under Bonita's coat, setting off a cloud of steam as the warm water met the cold, dense air.

Kerry Anne hesitated for a moment then yelled, "Help! Help! The pregnant ladies water broke!!"

Judy Larson was pouring coffee from a fresh pot she had just brewed on the open fire. Hearing Kerry Anne's cry for help she carefully set the pot down, and broke into a sprint across the ice, to help the women she had given a free cookie to earlier. As she slipped and slid over the frozen surface she yelled to her husband, "Jerry, tell the Sheriff to radio the hospital, we got a baby coming!"

Kerry Anne stood fascinated watching Bonita squirm and writhe back and forth, as though she is making a snow angel, but the agitating up and down was rather unfitting for such a saintly reproduction. Judy reached the scene in time to witness a very strange event about to unfold. Ice crystals began to form on the folds of Bonita's coat and she let out a very unladylike grunt. Kerry Anne and Judy stood shoulder to shoulder as their eyes grew as big as saucers watching the spectacle, known as Bonita, before them. Without hesitation, Judy cupped her hands around her mouth for a make-shift microphone and yelled out to her husband once more, "Cancel the hospital and radio The National Inquirer! This woman just gave birth to, what looks to be, a six-pound Walleye."

Tyrone heard the commotion, and snapped out of his stupor. Turning his attention away from Goldie, he gazed for a frozen moment watching Bonita's gyrations on the ice. He dropped Goldie's fishing stick; making a run for it. He'd hoped he could make it back to his pickup, and leave the scene without getting caught. His weight, and the ridges on his boots, gave him pretty good traction as he skimmed over the lake. But what Tyrone didn't know was that Jerry had lettered in shotput in high school. Picking up a ten-gallon Igloo cooler, Jerry threw it about fifty feet, hitting Tyrone right in the back of his head throwing him off balance, landing him face down sliding right into Denny Benson's fishing spot. A small group of men, who had been watching the tumultuous incident, shuffled over and tackle Tyrone. Denny then reached into his tackle box and pulled out a pair of handcuffs, to which he clamped onto Tyrone's wrists. Eyebrows were raised, but no one inquired why Denny had the cuffs.

Bonita's winter coat was ridged and inflexible in the cold, making it difficult for her to rise to her feet. As soon as she did, Judy took ahold of her arm; marching her over to the registration table. Bonita started sniveling, which prompted Judy to begin her oration, "Oh don't you be crying to me; you get what you deserve. If I were your mother, I'd be so ashamed. Cheating at a fishing contest, what's the world coming to!"

Kerry Anne held the walleye close to her like a new born baby; shuffling it over to the registration's stock tank, and slipped it in. Bonita and Tyrone now sat silently in the back seat of the sheriff's car. Their bucket and fishing stick remained abandoned by the hole in the ice.

Goldie, Kerry Anne and I hung out until the contest was over, eating cookies and drinking coffee. An old timer, named Harry Gustafson, won the contest with a four pound Northern. The Forest Lake Times reporter was at the scene taking pictures. "I don't need no picture," Harry said.

Pointing to Kerry Anne, Goldie and me, Harry winked and said, "Those three should get the glory."

We hit the front page of Monday's edition; Harry Gustafson's picture, holding the winning fish, was on page 3.

## CHAPTER THIRTY-SEVEN

# TRICK QUESTION

**A**fter the fishing tournament, I dropped Goldie off at her house; continuing on to mine to drop off the pick-up, and change into my other clothes. Before heading back to the flat, my mom asked if I would be staying the night, and having Sunday dinner the next day with her and my dad. This was a trick question. It had been my mother's hope that on any weekend I may be home she would bring me to confession, so that I may attend Mass the following Sunday, and receive "Holy Communion" with a pure soul. Having been duped into this before, I planned my strategy in advance. I gave her a reason to get back to the city, in hopes that I wouldn't hurt her feelings. I knew she had my best interest at heart. She'd been brow beaten with Catholicism her whole life, and worried endlessly for my soul in the afterlife.

But living on my own gave me freedom I never had as a child. Now weekends took on a whole new meaning, I had no job to get to and could stay in my pajamas for the entire day, if I wanted. I indulged myself with watching TV, eating popcorn until I was sick, and watched reruns of old movies on TV all day; my favorite was Laurel and Hardy. This was the freedom I had been waiting for since the age of fifteen; by that time I was pretty much churched out, and catholicized beyond belief.

As far back as I could remember as a child; every Sunday was the same. My siblings and I would get up, put on our "Sunday" clothes, and be ready to head out the door by 8:45, so we would be sure of getting a good seat at church for the 9:15 mass. My father, a Lutheran, sitting at the kitchen table drinking coffee, had no intention of joining us. He hated the Catholic Church, often complaining about the Pope residing in the Vatican with all his jewels, while people starved in the streets of Vatican City. My mother thought the Pope had a one-on-one connection with God, and prayed for my father's soul. Unless we children were dying, we never missed mass on Sunday.

In second grade the dutiful ritual of church was extended by adding Saturday Catechism classes. I would sit with other second graders from 9am to 11, floundering in a classroom. Teachers of the faith forever etched in our brains the Our Father, Hail Mary, and The Apostles Creed.

Objective: to learn how to be a good Catholic. I hated it! Catholicism engulfed my whole being. Staying up late on a Saturday night was forbidden. "We have church in the morning," was a phrase I grew to hate.

Second grade level of Catechism upgraded the Catholic for preparation to receive the sacrament of Holy Communion. For girls, the anticipation of wearing white Patent leather shoes, white anklet socks, and a white dress with a veil was something to look forward to, and envied by most Protestant girls. The boys attire would be less exciting, wearing white shirts with clip-on bow ties, corduroy pants, and spit shined shoes. They would get fresh haircuts for the occasion; usually a short, tapered style with a small tuft of hair left on top for a dollop of hair cream. The boys appeared less excited about the event, but followed protocol under duress.

We were taught the Ten Commandments; expected to recite each one in any given order and give the meaning. We were never quizzed on the Tenth Commandment. "Thou shalt not covet thy neighbor's wife." We just needed to know we shouldn't do it. "Do what?" we would ask but never get an answer. Confusing children didn't seem to bother teachers of the faith. It bothered me.

Catholics were going to make it into heaven, regardless of any unsavory foregoing. Their loop hole: Confession.

Webster's definition: Confess' v. 1. Admit (crime) 2. Tell (one's sins) confession.

Confession for the catholic was not only essential, but mandatory, in making your First Communion. We were told how wonderful confession was going to be. Through the power of the Priest we could release our sins to God; making our souls pure again. If you weren't sure what horrible sins you might have done to blacken your soul in your first seven years of life, believe you me, the Catholic educator of guilt would remind you.

Making my first confession scared the crap out of me. I had been preparing for this moment for months, and now the time had arrived; our catechism class was coached for the final time Saturday morning, and that evening would be the moment to clean our souls.

After dinner that night my mom piled me and my siblings into the car. Our dad, the biggest sinner of us all, stayed at home. In our catholic teachings, if you were protestant you wouldn't be allowed into heaven anyway.

We moved into church behind our mother; like ducklings off to the pond. All was going well as we entered the vestibule. My mother glanced over us with a final inspection; stopping dead in her tracks before opening the second set of doors.

Looking at me she says, "Where's your scarf!?"

"I left it at home."

Before entering the church, it was essential for all women to cover their heads with a hat or scarf. My mother wore a black meshwork held together by little tufts of black fuzz created in a circular pattern. In Vogue it was quite fashionable; to me it resembled a spider web at best. She quickly dug into her pocketbook; pulling out a tissue; removed a bobby pin from the mesh; attaching the tissue to the top of my head. I had just advanced from child, to devout confessing catholic wearing my tissue shroud. I was now acceptable in the eyes of the church to be allowed to enter. Men, on the other hand, had to remove their hats. I'm in second grade and I think this is the biggest line of malarkey I've heard so far.

A few lights were lit at the back of the church, with a few votive candles that flickered in the front, by the statue of the Blessed Virgin Mary. The confessionals were located in the back of the church, against the wall. Three doors, side by side, entered into three closet-size rooms. The center closet was for the priest, and housed a comfortable chair. The two confessionals bordering each side were for the sinners. We knelt on a rectangular wooden box that would face us towards the sliding wooden door with a screen in front of it. When the moment of reckoning arrived, the Priest would slide the wooden door to the side with a bang. There was no mistake, it was show time!

Without hesitation, my mother led us to the line already in progress, formed against the wall under stained glass windows of the Stations of the Cross. Those coming out of the confessional would go directly to a pew, kneel and silently say the prayers of their penance. Some weren't so silent and their mumbling echoed throughout the building. An occasional cough, or blowing of a nose made anyone under the age of ten want to giggle.

Travis Martin was waiting in line five people ahead of me. He was the meanest boy in school. I despised him. Maybe being malicious was his defense mechanism. Maybe he feared being teased because he had one nostril larger than the other. None the less, I thought he had the personality of a stick. He liked to beat up first graders and was continually called to the office at school. Nothing ever changed. His parents were well known in the community and Travis's punishment was always short term. Once he was off the hook, he was back terrorizing the first graders. Travis would twist some kids arm, or trip them playing basketball. Once again, he would be hauled off to the principal's office. There he sat, until recess was over and the bell rang. Upon returning to class he'd always sported a smart-ass grin. We all knew he would be back at it, the next chance he got.

Standing in line, I tried to remain focused on the task at hand. Travis leaned out from the wall and looked back at me mouthing the word "Swine." He was disgusting. I thought he would take forever in the confessional, given his history. But I was wrong. He was out in mere minutes, said his penance in less than thirty seconds and left. He lived across the street from the church so there wasn't any parent to answer to. I'm thinking in his entire life there was never anyone to answer to.

I was now standing two sinners away from the confessional. Running some sins through my head, I feared a mental block coming on. I learned in Catechism I should confess three sins and to pick the worst.

1. Broke the fifth commandment; Honor thy Father & Mother. I didn't eat the lima beans in my vegetable soup and fed them to our dog, Spooky, waiting under the table. He was a black lab and we loved him. He would eat anything, except raw carrots.

2. Broke the fifth again; didn't brush my teeth, when I said I did.

3. Broke the fifth again; threw a rock at my brother and denied I did it.

I felt all my actions were justified. I figured once I grew up, and didn't have my parents telling me what to do, I would no longer have a reason to confess anything. It made perfect sense to me.

The moment had arrived. It was now my turn to enter the dark closet of admission. I panicked, what if someone opens the door when I'm in the middle of confessing? What if I forget what to say? I was temporarily frozen in place, until my mom gave me a slight nudge on my shoulder to go in. I entered the black hole. With fear twisting at my stomach, I looked back at my mom; she motioned for me to close the door. What if it gets stuck, I thought, and they have to call the fire department? Oh great, now I needed to go to the bathroom. I crossed my legs, giving mom the sign that I needed to go; she gave me "that look," like if I didn't get on with it, there would be consequences.

I entered, closed the door, knelt and waited. The priest was listening to the confession from the other side. I could hear everything! I was so caught up in the conversation that when the sliding wooden window banged open, I jumped out of my skin blurting, "Holy Jesus! I mean cow...cow."

I could see the silhouette of Father Strat, "continue," he mumbled. I started my confession and made it all the way to the second offense, but now I was drawing a blank.

"Anything else?" Father Strat asked.

"I can't remember," I answered nervously.

"Very well," he mumbled; continuing with words of absolution and the sign of the cross.

So that was it. I made it! I now had my first confession under my belt. Tomorrow would be the big day; I would make my first Holy Communion. Tomorrow I would eat the body and blood of Christ in the form of a wafer. I tried not to think about it. Before this, cannibalism was only talked about in Tarzan movies. We would be required to fast at least three hours before church. If you didn't fast for three hours before communion you would be creating a sin, punishable by Catholic guilt. On a hot summer day, in a church packed like sardines, people would drop like flies from dehydration and hunger. Strong men would hurry to the rescue, taking the unconscious to the church basement to cool off and recover amongst the cool cement walls.

I had a restless night's sleep; waking to a morning of no food. Luckily the sun was shining and the weather was perfect for my catechism class to gather outside the church, before making our entrance. We filed in, girls on the left and boys on the right. We sat in the pews reserved the same way. Girl's left, boy's right. We sat until Father Strat entered from a side door, with an altar boy on each side. Facing his flock, he lifted his arms to heaven; we rose obediently; then he made an outward sign of the cross and said: "In no'mine Patris, et Filii, et Spiritus Sancti Amen."

We were told this meant: "In the name of the Father, the Son and the Holy Spirit." We had no other interpretation from this point on. We sat obediently, listening to the Latin mass, not having a clue.

The communion rail separated the altar from the congregation, standing about three feet high with kneelers in front. The moment had arrived and we filed in formation, hands in prayer position, knelt, cocked our heads back, and stuck out our tongues like birds waiting for a worm. Mass ended shortly after that, and we gathered in the church basement for our celebratory breakfast. The long banquet tables were set in a U shape with Father Strat sitting at the head. Next to Father Strat was Travis Martin. Rumor had it, he had planned to be an Altar Boy.

I sat next to Jeanie E. She was Polish and I couldn't pronounce her last name. We were best friends and could talk about anything. While we were eating our toast and scrambled eggs, I asked her what she thought of communion.

"It was wonderful; I can't wait to do it again," she said.

"The wafer stuck to the roof of my mouth; I just got it lose with my orange juice," I said.

"Did you see God?" she asked me.

"God!?" I was shocked, "No, did you?"

"Yep, I closed my eyes real tight and he appeared in my brain." She told me.

I was speechless. I saw nothing. I casually finished my breakfast, looking at Travis Martin sitting next to Father Strat. Humph, Altar Boy? The irony of life amazed me.

CHAPTER THIRTY-EIGHT

# ALL POINTS BULLETIN

I was totally zapped from my day in the cold air and tournament dealings. Finbar picked me up at my parents as planned; with hugs and kisses goodbye from my folks, and a brown paper sack of peanut butter cookies for both of us, we were on our way back to the city. I fell asleep for the ride back to Minneapolis; Finbar woke me when we arrive at Garfield Flats.

"Would you like to come in for a while?" I asked. "You could go to the parade with us."

"Nah, got some studying to do," he said, as he grabbed me for a good-bye hug.

"Catch ya later," I said over my shoulder as I hopped out of his car. Always the gentleman, Finbar waited for me to get inside the building before he drove off.

I had just enough time to change my clothes and grab a quick bite, before heading out for the Torchlight Parade. As soon as I unlocked the door to 4G I was hit head on with Debbie in a panic. I gave myself a moment to reflect on how my mother would handle this particular situation before reacting. Then I tried my best to calm her down.

"Slow down, slow down, what's going on?" I took her by the elbow and escorted her over to the couch. "Sit down and take a deep breath.....start from the beginning."

"Mrs. Winningham called," she gasped, "We all have to report for duty."

"Oh my god, she has finally gone total military. Doesn't she realize it's Saturday? And what do you mean by all?"

"Everyone from Unit Control, Mrs. Odettes needs our help." Debbie continues, The Daughters of Norway came down with the flu. The only ones that aren't sick are Mrs. Odette's and Sully. Mrs. Winningham said we have to hurry to Sully's garage. She wants us to fill in for the Daughters and be the Norski's on the float. Mrs. Winningham will have the costumes waiting for all of us and whoever fits what, we wear. From that point on all's we have to do is smile and wave. Thank God you got home in time; Alice will be picking us up any minute."

Now, it was one thing to help Mrs. Odette's with the float, but the fact that I'm Swedish and will now have to pose as a Norski, well that's just sacrilegious. I kept my bigotry to myself, knowing this insensitivity would be Greek to my Greek roommate.

## CHAPTER THIRTY-NINE

# THE BEST LAID PLANS

**M**rs. Odettes had been so excited with anticipation for the night of the Torchlight Parade. Now that it had finally arrived, everything was going wrong. The Daughters had the flu and she feared Celia may not be able to reach any of the girls from Unit Control. Her fear of disaster was overwhelming her; the idea that the float might be driven through the streets empty, with no participants, had her nervous and flustered.

She kept a bottle of valium in her medicine cabinet for emergencies. Her doctor prescribed them the day she set her hair on fire, trying to light a cigarette. Oftentimes her osteoporosis played havoc with her life, igniting her hair was one of them. She had taken one valium when she first got the news that the Daughters of Norway were sick and couldn't make it. She still felt stressed and the dosage specifically said to only take one pill every six hours. It was too soon to take another pill, but she needed to shake the uneasiness building up inside her. She thought perhaps a shot of Irish whiskey would help. She would then get ready to go and call a cab.

## CHAPTER FORTY

# DRESSING THE PART

Celia Winningham was in her element. On more than one occasion, during our decorating of the float, she wanted to take over command, but her respect for Mrs. Odettes kept her in her place. Now time was of the essence; Mrs. Odettes had yet to show up. Celia had Sully check all the wires and the generator on the float, making sure the lights and microphones were working. The convertible was hooked up to the flatbed with its velvet blanket in place for the King and Queen to sit upon. She then instructed Sully to take her car and retrieve the Norwegian Royalty, waiting at the St. Paul Hilton.

When Debbie and I arrived the costumes were waiting, piled in a heap on the front of the float; starting with traditional folk dresses with embroidered shawls and bonnets, in deep red and indigo on the top. Like soldiers in the military, we obediently lined up shoulder to shoulder so Celia could move quickly, holding each costume up for sizing. I was relieved that I was too tall, as usual, for the dresses. Debbie was too short, so Alice and Patty got the honors of being the Norski women in the cottage.

Next on the heap was a tattered outfit of brown baggy pants, heavy overcoat, and fur hat with earmuffs; a pair of gloves with the ends of the fingers cut off completed the ensemble. It fit Celia's corpulent figure perfectly. The last costumes on the heap were two very peculiar looking, large, rubber fish heads. One was a pink Salmon, with huge eyes and a mouth open just enough to see out of. The other was a black and silver cod, with rubbery scales on the cheeks under its small squinty eyes. It also had an open mouth to look through. Each head came with a matching jump suit. Debbie and I were stymied, staring in disbelief.

"I guess these will go to you two." Celia said with a roguish grin.

Something led us to believe the costumes had been strategically piled for dispensing. Debbie and I look at the heads, turning to Celia in disbelief.

"I'm not wearing that!" Debbie pouted.

"This is not the time to be challenging." Celia was adamant, "Do it for Mrs. Odettes," she said laying on the guilt.

"Where **is** Mrs. Odettes?" We all asked in unison.

"I'm not sure. If she doesn't show, we'll have to go ahead as planned without her," Celia instructed, "we have no choice."

The jumpsuits were the same size but with Debbie's passion for pink, she immediately went for the Salmon. I, not giving a crap anymore, took the Cod. Debbie's suit was too long in the torso and the legs puddle around her ankles, making her look more like a deformed Manatee than a Salmon. Mine fit me short in the legs, barely making it to my ankles, with the torso cinching tightly on my body. If I had balls, they would be Norski indigo by now. We put on the rubber fish heads, adjusting them so we could see through the tiny holes. A moment of silence moved over the group.

"You look good in Pink, Debbie," Patty said cynically.

"Do you want to live to see Monday? One more crack and I'll deck you with my crutch. I've had practice ya know." Debbie's voice was slightly muffled under the rubber hood, but her annoyance came through loud and clear.

"OK, that's enough. Everyone take your places, it's almost time to go," Celia ordered.

"There's just one problem," Alice stated, "What are we supposed to sing? I can't sing in Norwegian. I can barely hold a tune for Happy Birthday."

"Sing some Christmas songs," Celia snorted.

"Christmas is over," Patty chortled, realizing too late she had just gotten on Celia's last nerve.

"I don't care if you mime at this point, just get on the damn float and park it in the cottage!" Celia Winningham, for the first time in front of her crew, had lost all composure and was freaking out. At that moment Sully pulled into the garage with the King and Queen. They knew enough English to exchange some niceties, and with Sully's help, climbed into the back of the convertible. Sully closed the passenger door, and as he rounded the front of the car to get in the driver's side, barfed like he just ate Lutefisk for the first time.

We all looked on in disbelief. With no time to waste, Sully gave Celia the directions as to where to get in line for the parade. It was only a short distance from his garage, but we still had no Mrs. Odettes and time was running out.

Patty and Alice took their positions in the cottage. I stood by the mock berm of snow; Debbie sat on the bench in front of the ice shanty, placing her crutches in front of her. Mrs. Winningham got behind the wheel of the convertible, looking like a vagabond involved in grand theft auto.

It had been years since Mrs. Winningham had driven a stick. There were no bucket seats back then; just a bench seat with a four in the floor. She had been driving automatics for such a long time, she had forgotten the adrenalin rush she used to get working the clutch and gas, letting the car know she was in charge. She looked at the Bakelite gearshift knob, with the four-speed pattern on the top, and calmly wrapped her right hand around it. She placed one foot on the clutch and the other on the gas; giving it a little pump, revving the engine, brought it to life. Sully managed to open the garage door and Mrs. Winningham coaxed the shift into first gear, slowly releasing the clutch, simultaneously pressing on the gas, transferring torque from the engine to the transmission. At first it was a chug and a jerk forward. Once we were on the main road, and in second gear, the ride became a little smoother.

We made it over to Wacouta Street, following Sully's instructions to pull in behind the Shriners Bag Pipe ensemble. So far Alice and Patty were unable to think of anything to sing, and decide they would just smile and wave. The King and Queen were sitting in position on the trunk of the car, with part of the velvet blanket wrapped around their legs. It was a cold ride, even though Celia had the heat on full blast. Debbie and I agreed the rubber fish heads were advantageous; protecting our faces from the bitter wind chill, and hiding our identity from any possible acquaintances attending the parade.

It was now 5:30 and the lights of the parade loomed in the darkness far ahead. I got a rush of butterflies in my stomach thinking back to when I attended this parade as a child. Our float slowly moved as best as Celia could keep in sync with the other attendees. The King and Queen finally smiled, waving enthusiastically to the crowd. Patty was showing Alice how to wave like a princess, something she had been practicing since Homecoming 1967. Debbie and I decided we would just nod. I swayed from side to side while Debbie sat motionless on the bench in front of the fishing shanty. Being that fish weren't supposed to have arms, we didn't feel it was necessary to wave.

We reached Fifth Street, and about to make the first turn, when Mrs. Odettes hopped out of a taxi cab that was parked at the corner. Patty and Alice quit waving, I quit nodding and swaying and Debbie looked frozen like a lawn ornament left out for the winter. As soon as Celia saw Mrs. Odettes she slammed on the breaks, forgetting to step on the clutch, killed the motor, causing the car to chug and stop dead in its tracks, making the King and Queen topple forward into a heap in the back seat.

We all watched in disbelief as Mrs. Odettes scooted across the slippery street dressed as the most astonishing leprechaun we had ever seen. Mrs. Odettes was green and sparkly from head to toe! Her top hat glistened against the float's string of lights; her fitted tuxedo jacket was tailored precisely to flare at her hips; her knickers were a shiny satin with argon socks pulled up to her knees; her black buckled shoes look very similar to a pilgrims and gave her very little traction. She ran, she slipped, she slid, and with a loud, "whoop, whoop, oh no!" she made it to the side of the float without falling. She tried to hop on, but her tiny body, slippery shoes, and the constrictive nature of her fitted suit, made it unmanageable to get the momentum she needed to make the leap. I quickly hopped off the flatbed and gave her a boost while Debbie handed her a crutch to grab on to. "On the count of two!" I yelled. We didn't have time to count to three.

Celia restarted the car while the King and Queen climbed up, back onto the velvet blanketed trunk. We had fallen a block behind the Shriners and needed to make up for lost time. With four speed positraction, Celia had underestimated the power when given too much torque and by the time I hit the number two on the count, Celia planted the rear tires into the pavement, Debbie gave a mighty pull on the crutch, tumbling backward from the force of the car, sending Mrs. Odettes sailing across the slippery Ivory Snow Flakes, like Sparky the seal hopping out of the pool at Como Zoo. The King and Queen land flat on their backs and I barely had time to hop back on the float.

Mrs. Odettes crashed into the cottage, after flattening part of the papier mache berm, thus coating her leprechaun outfit with more glitter and sparkles than a mirror ball. Debbie and I commented how we had never seen a human hydroplane before. Patty and Alice tried to get out of the cottage to help Mrs. Odettes up, but she was sitting in a disoriented lump in front of the door. Debbie and I ran across the float lake and pulled Mrs. Odettes out of the way so Patty and Alice could escape. We were unable to get Mrs. Odettes to her feet. Debbie and I took a hold of each hand, Alice and Patty each took a foot, and we carried her into the cottage, out of sight.

Celia was trying to see what is happening, but the King and Queen obstructed her view in the rearview mirror, the only thing visible were two very disgruntled members of royalty. She had no choice but to drive on, staying with the momentum of the parade.

It was obvious Mrs. Odettes wasn't her same old self. Her eyes were drooping at half-mast and her speech was somewhat slurred. She was oblivious to the fact she was wearing the wrong costume and none of us thought we should mention it. She was agreeable to the idea of sitting in the cottage to rest a bit. Patty and Alice helped position Mrs. Odettes by propping her in the corner, then returned outside, standing by the door holding her hostage. They resumed their waving like nothing had happened. I took hold of Debbie's uncrutched arm, shuffling back over to the bench.

"What a cluster fuck." Debbie garbled under her rubber fish head.

"Well, at least only a few people saw her. We only have a few more blocks to go, should be smooth sailing the rest of the way," I said reassuringly.

"Smooth Sailing! You're kidding, right? Did that fish costume bless you with a mariners' quick guide to parading? Smooth sailing my ass! Nothing has gone smooth in weeks! I hardly think tonight will present any miracles!" Debbie's voice thundered from under the rubber hood. She nodded her head from side to side, undoubtedly she was becoming unglued. Not wanting to exacerbate the situation any more than necessary, I agreed with her and gave her a fish head nod.

"What exactly does that mean?" She barked at me.

"I nodded... It means yes...no...wait...it means I'm freezing my ass off in the rubber head! Yikes woman, what do you think it means?...you need to chill!" I had had more than enough fresh air for the day; my toes were becoming numb; I was getting tired, and my usually calm demeanor was beginning to waver.

We had just passed Wabasha Street when the Shriners started playing their ever-popular tune of Danny Boy, on the bagpipes. A rustling sound had begun to emerge from the speakers positioned on the roof of our floats cottage. At first we had all forgotten about the sound system, but were quickly reminded as we watched in disbelief. A sparkling green leprechaun slowly escalated like an apparition in the cottage window. Mrs. Odettes was on the second verse by the time she was in full view. Hanging slightly over the edge of the cottage window, she broke into tears as she accompanied the bag pipes singing *"tis you, tis you must go and I must bide"* ending with a hiccup that set her off balance, making her sink back into the cottage and out of sight.

Debbie and I remained at the bench in silence, deciding it would be a good time to start waving.

Patty and Alice disappeared into the cottage to check on Mrs. Odettes. Seconds later Patty came out and hysterically scurried across to our side.

"We don't know what to do!" Patty shrieked, with tears freezing halfway down her rosy cheeks.

"Just stay with her until the parade is over. We just passed Rice Park; I think we end at Market Street." I responded.

"You don't understand," Patty started wheezing, becoming more frantic, "Mrs. Odettes is dead."

Debbie and I faced each other and in unison mutter, "Shit."

At this point we had totally forgotten there is even a parade going on. Following Patty, we hustled across the lake to the cottage, not having any idea what could be done. When we opened the cottage door Alice was praying over the body and weeping, saying things like, "she was such a dear friend" and "such a sad way to go."

Debbie handed me her fish head and bent down on her knees next to Mrs. Odettes.

"Maybe there's a chance we can get her to the hospital." She grabbed Mrs. Odettes wrist but the bitter cold made Debbie's fingers too numb, impossible to detect a pulse. She then unbuttoned the top button of the leprechaun tuxedo and leaned in to rest her ear on Mrs. Odettes heart. But something cold and hard under the leprechaun vest stopped Debbie from going any further. She reached in, pulling out an empty fifth of whiskey.

"She's not dead! She's shit faced, drunk, passed out cold!" Debbie exclaimed.

We made it to Market Street, where the Torchlight Parade had come to an end. Mrs. Odettes recovered enough for Celia to put her in a cab, sending her back home. The King and Queen of Norway were appalled at the evenings events, and didn't even give us a wave goodbye as they sped off in a cab, back to the Hilton. Alice, Patty, Debbie, Celia and I piled into the convertible, cranked up the heat, and headed back to Sully's garage. With the top down the breeze was sharp, but Debbie and I rode contentedly under our fish head cupolas.

No one showed up for work on Monday...or Tuesday...or Wednesday. We all came down with the flu and the Unit Control Department was in recovery.

## CHAPTER FORTY-ONE

# PARADE PRIDE

"The Daughters of Norway" didn't win the first prize as they had hoped. They hired Sully to fix the boiler and started planning their strategy for next year's float. The float did place third and the Daughters were complimented, by the Carnival Committee, that it was very clever and entertaining the way the Leprechaun was worked into the Scandinavian theme, singing Danny Boy so beautifully with the Shriners. Third place prize was the use of the Como Park Pavilion for a Summer Day picnic. It was unanimous by The Daughters of Norway, that Mrs. Odettes and the Unit Control Department use the award.

## CHAPTER FORTY-TWO

# LIFE GOES ON

Life had returned to normalcy. Winter was over and spring was blooming everywhere. Our flat had been peaceful since Bonita and Tyrone moved out; with the help of a police escort. Debbie had returned to her old self with poufy hair, sexy eyes, the latest fashions, and Renekee by her side. They were getting along like two peas in a pod. We took down the tie-died sheets and hung real curtains. We put the beads in the lost-and-found box in the laundry room; they were gone in less than twenty-four hours. Our flat no longer smelled of incense, but from time to time, had a hint of Emeraude perfume. I still hadn't spent my hundred dollars from betting on the race and proposed an idea to Debbie.

"What do you think of moving someplace else?" I asked her. "We can use my gambling money for the deposit."

"Don't you like it here anymore?" She questioned me with a curious look.

"I'm kind of over it. You know? Maybe get something above ground. Too much left over bad karma here."

"I thought you didn't believe in karma?" She asked with a puzzled look, slightly smirking.

"That was before the flower children showed up. Now I have developed a completely different perspective."

"Well, now that you mention it, our lease will be up soon. I could dig moving to a new place. After all, life's a poop shoot." Debbie agreed.

"Crapshoot." I add, "Life's a crapshoot. So, you don't want to run this by Renekee first?"

Debbie giggled, "NO, he's not the boss of me."

I'm relieved by her response. "That settles it; the search for our new place begins!"

CHAPTER FORTY-THREE

# GOODBYE TO ALICE

It was decided by Mrs. Odette's to use her third-place prize as a sendoff for her very good friend and co-worker Alice. It was a perfect, warm, sunny Sunday in June, Como Park Pavilion was the perfect setting. We each brought a dish to share, Mrs. Odettes brought the beverage. Debbie and I hoped she would put a little dash of Irish whiskey in it, but no such luck. Sully was thrilled to participate and offered to be our grill master. Our guest of honor, Alice, was beaming and excited to begin her life as a full-time mom. Her husband, George, tried to visit with everyone as much as possible, but needed to keep a watchful eye on his son, Alejandro, who could crawl faster than most people could walk and could eat a bug in ten seconds or less. It was the perfect send off to part of our work family, yet bittersweet.

## CHAPTER FORTY-FOUR

# THE REPLACEMENT

O n Monday morning, the Unit Control Department was feeling melancholy with the departure of Alice. Everyone was working diligently at their desks, without the usual social chatter of the past weekend. Mrs. Winningham announced that after lunch the new girl, who was to replace Alice, would be stopping in to meet everyone. We all tried to appear happy, but we all agreed the feeling was remorseful. When lunchtime rolled around Patty went early with Mrs. Odettes. When they returned Debbie and I headed over to Walgreens for a grilled cheese and fries.

I brought Sunday's classified ads with me so we could go over available apartments in the Uptown area. We each took a section, and began to scan the columns.

"Here's one," I said as I circled the ad, "two bedrooms, kitchen and dining combo, no pets. It's located above Bridgeman's ice cream shop. What do you think?"

"Sounds ok," Debbie said as she grabbed a fry from my plate, "it could be risky for our figures though. Listen to this one: Stewardess with Northwest Airlines looking to share an apartment with one or two other women. Then it lists a local phone number here and when to call. If we got another girl to split the rent, we could get a bigger place. What do you think? Should we call her?"

We both agreed it was definitely worth considering an extra person to share the rent. We finished our lunch and headed back to Unit Control. As we entered the office area, a young figure of a women was sitting in Alice's chair. She had chestnut brown hair and judging from behind I could see she had a tiny waist. A seductive slit in her skirt exposed a shapely leg.

"Girls," Mrs. Winningham announced upon our return, "I'd like to introduce you to our new member of Unit Control, Sharon Provili."

Sharon stood up from Alice's chair, turned around, and with the look of surprise squealed, "MIAAAA."

Debbie looked at me and mouthed the word, "damn."

"Hello, Jackal" I sneered, "I didn't know your name was Sharon."

## CHAPTER FORTY-FIVE

# MOVING ON

Debbie made the call, setting up a time to meet the Stewardess. After work, we were to head over to twenty second and Pillsbury Avenue, not far from Garfield Flats. We hopped the 17, optimistic of a possible new adventure. Debbie gave me a long look and then commented, "I have to say Mia, when you called Sharon by her pseudo name, I was shocked but impressed. The look on Celia's face was priceless, but couldn't compare to the look on Jackal's!"

"I've had enough of that bitch" I replied.

"Wow! I do believe I'm rubbing off on you." Debbie commented with a note of pleasure.

"Yep, fasten your seat belts it's going to be a bumpy night," I said.

"Tonight's going to be bumpy?" she asked. "You mean with Jackal, right? Working with her will be bumpy."

"You're catching on Debbie. I do believe I'm rubbing off on you."

*COMING SOON:*

# CONVENT CONDO

Turn the page to enjoy a sample of the next installment of Mia Carlson's pursuit of adulthood, trying to find herself, regardless of how difficult and unfamiliar it is.

**CONVENT CONDO – Coming out soon!**

# Convent Condo

## CHAPTER ONE

# ON THE COUCH

I sat uncomfortably in an overstuffed chair of worn-out maroon velvet. It looked like it would have been relaxing to sink in to, but we all know how looks can be deceiving. It was another baking hot, summer day; the curtain on the office window was drawn shut. A desk lamp expelled its manufactured light and heat that made the room a redundant scenario for, what was supposed to be, a place of theoretical tranquility. I'm not a patient; I want you to know.

I became bored with flipping through magazines of nothing important. I stood from my slump the chair had forced me into, straightened away the creases in my skirt, adjusted my zipper, aligning it with the center of my left hip, and re-tucked my blouse. My anxiety was overwhelming; I started pacing the floor. Now… the room was gray. I glanced at the velvet chair, as though it had a soul. Was it watching me? It had changed its color to emerald green and the worn patches on its arms are now shiny new. Piano music came from down the hall. I recognized the simple prelude that now paralleled my loss of reality.

The door opened and startled me from my pacing. The man I'd been expecting had finally arrived. Approaching me without a word, he gently placed his hands at my waist, pulling me in closer to him. His eyes were striking blue against our shadowed surroundings. His lips touched mine gently at first, then deeper. The music kept playing and my heart beat unconsciously in time as we simultaneously moved our way toward a crescendo. I found it impossible to focus. I was consumed by his strength as he lifted me, holding me in his arms. Instinctively I embrace him, as his mouth moved over my flesh, biting me ever so gently, igniting the heat within.

"Where do we go from here?" I asked, but he didn't answer. The colors were gone now and the face that gazed at me had changed. Everything had changed....

"What?! What are you doing?" I asked, irritated that it's the middle of the night and my roommate's nocturnal lifestyle has interfered with my slumber, as she stumbled about in search of something in my room.

"Sorry, I was looking for the TV guide," she whispered.

"In the first place, it's the middle of the night; I doubt there is anything on TV. Second, I don't have a TV in here. AND third, I was asleep!" She got the hint that she may have overstepped her boundaries, and left my room.

Three women living together will at times stir an occasional confrontation. Our joint relationship began when Debbie and I replied to an ad in the classifieds.

CHAPTER TWO

# A NEW PLACE TO LIVE

**D**ebbie and I had agreed to meet Misty after work. We got off the bus at Nicollet and Twenty Second Street, only two blocks from our destination. The address sounded familiar at the time, however, overlooked by our anticipation of sharing an apartment with a stewardess, and the potential to boost our rank on the ladder of peer approval. Pondering on the address was inconsequential, or so we thought. Our chatter of what was to be soon came to a halt, along with our heightened step. We stood speechless looking at the remarkably large, white building sitting ominously on the corner, taking up half a block.

The sun had just gone behind the clouds, and what had been a breeze now shifted its direction, picking up momentum. Shielding my eyes from the dirt churning about I said, "I can't believe this! Can you?" Debbie didn't answer. "What's with this weather?! I continued, "Debbie, did you think it was going to be this place?" Still shielding my eyes, I peeked through my fingers. She still didn't answer. "Debbie," I said as I turned to look at her. She had made an about-face and was headed back to Nicollet. Quickly I ran after her grabbing her arm, while I hung on to my skirt from the gusting wind.

"I'm not going in there," she shouted adamantly, as if I were hard of hearing. Squinting to keep the dirt from piercing her vision she persisted, "I'm just fine with Garfield Flats."

"We can't just leave Misty without at least talking to her! She's probably waiting inside now."

"Sure," Debbie said, "provided she's still alive."

The three-story building could have used a new coat of paint on its weathered, clapboard siding. A row of leaded glass windows faced the alley and could be seen from where we were standing. The same types of windows were duplicated on the second story, suggesting a similar floor plan. The raised attic had two large dormers with paned windows, and an old weather vane perched atop the peak of the structure, trundling out of control. Ever since we had lived in the Uptown area, we had heard about the haunted convent. How ghosts of nuns roamed the building; how tenants would see objects moving in the night. It was rumored no renter ever fulfilled their lease, forfeiting their deposit just to get out. We had agreed to meet Misty inside the foyer of the North side entrance, by the mailboxes. In our arguing, we detected the silhouette of a person behind the leaded glass windows on the first floor; before it moved from view.

Debbie pointed to the first-floor leaded glass window, "Did you see that?! What the heck was that?! We need to get out of here, bad karma!" She was rattled and becoming unglued.

"Come on, it's just rumors, right? It was probably the landlord. We can do this. Who says we have to rent it? Maybe Misty has a list of other places to see." I tried my best to convince and console my friend, and myself.

"Always the optimist, aren't you? Well you're not the boss of me!" She snapped and pulled her arm from mine.

"Your karma has been wrong before ya know." I blurted, knowing as soon as I said it I was in big trouble.

"Ok, fine. You got me this time. But if it's creepy in there, we're out of here, deal?"

"Deal." We hung on to each other as we bucked the wind, climbing the stairs to the heavy oak door.

With hesitation, I reached for the handle; expecting a spark of energy from the beyond to paralyze me with an electric snap. Debbie watched me closely, ready to bolt at any moment. To my relief there was nothing. "See... nothing," I said as my thumb pressed down on the lever and pushed the door open.

"What's nothing?" Misty asked. There was no doubt in our minds as to who she was. She stood at about five foot nine, in a short-sleeved polyester blue dress with a small pin of gold wings on her collar. She had perfectly coifed, coal black hair cut to chin length, complimenting her strong jaw-line. Her pink lipstick melded across flawless full lips; false eyelashes batted nonstop; and her nose was an exquisite creation of perfect genes. She was friendly in a coffee, tea, or me, sort of way.

"Nothing," Debbie and I responded simultaneously, feeling a bit more than juvenile.

"Well, I'm Misty," she said. Showing her worldly maturity, she extended her hand for a shake. Feeling awkward, Debbie and I responded. "So," she continued, "I picked up the key from the landlord. The place is empty so he said to feel free to look around. If we like it I can return with our deposit, pick up two more keys, and the place is ours!"

There was no lengthy conversation on what we did for a living, or what our likes and dislikes were. She needed someone to share the rent, and that was as far as the exchange had gone. I gazed around the foyer and questioned why there were only three mail boxes.

"This is one of three entrances," Misty answered. "I was told there are back doors for each condo and stairwells going all the way from the third floor, down to a full basement connecting the entire house. It's like underground passages. Isn't that wild!"

"Are we talking catacombs?" I said, tongue in cheek.

"You're joking….right?" Misty said without expecting a reply. I felt foolish at her lack of humor. She was about to insert the key when the door slowly opened to condo number one. "That's strange, it wasn't even locked," she remarked. We followed her, entering into a large living area. At the far wall was a fireplace, still dirty with old ashes. To the left were two large windows looking out onto Twenty Second Street and to the right was the entry to the hallway. We made our way across the hardwood floors, disregarding an occasional creak, and entered the dining room to the left. It had a built-in buffet across one wall and adjacent to that were the leaded glass windows we had seen while standing outside. I thought of the image we'd noticed from the street and looked at Debbie. Neither of us said a word. Across from the dining area was the first bedroom. It was quite large with two windows facing an alcove in the center of the building. A small garden area showed signs of what may have been a gathering spot. Patches of grass, in need of water, were among pebbles and sand that were whirling about in the wind. A rusted, steel arbor arched over a cement birdbath sitting beneath, empty and lonely for another time. The windows across the way had opaque curtains that were drawn. As we continued down the hall two more bedrooms were to the right, each with a window facing the broken garden. At the end of the hall was the bathroom complete with footed tub, and a pedestal sink with white, ceramic hot and cold handles and faucet. The floor was made of black and white tile, intricately laid in a weave pattern. A medicine cabinet was set into the plaster wall and had a faded mirror for its door. Hesitating, I opened it to see what might have been left behind: one small bottle of iodine, and a box of band aides. On the hallway wall, across from the bedrooms, was a square opening, much like a pass way for food. It had a bead-board door with metal hinges and a latch. Debbie opened it and commented, "Oh, this opens to the kitchen," and looking at a buzzer that was mounted on the wall next to it she said: "The nuns here must have been sequestered."

"It's cloistered," I corrected.

"Well excuse me," she whispered sarcastically. Debbie always had a hard time accepting any linguistic guidance from me. Misty appeared to be caught up in her own thoughts and not interested in our banter. We followed her like obedient school children and walked back down the hall and through the dining room to get into the kitchen. The room was larger than any kitchen I'd ever seen. Metal cabinets hung the full length of one wall, stopping at the square pass-way we had just peered through. A long counter and cabinets sat beneath. A newer stainless-steel sink was in the center of the counter and seemed out of place in its surroundings. Against the wall, next to the back door, was a large, white stove with two ovens side by side. On one half of the top were four coiling burners and on the other half was a metal cover sitting atop a built-in griddle. A silver plate with the manufactures name was attached to the back-splash, next to its clock, that was stopped at twelve thirty. "Do either of you cook?" Misty asked.

"Not really. Do you?" Debbie asked.

"Not really, but I love to bake." She said.

We followed Misty out the back door and paused momentarily in the stairwell. Looking out the back window, the wind continued to blow.

Misty paused and said, "That's so strange, I don't remember a storm in the forecast. Well, what do you think… shall we take a look at the basement?" Misty didn't wait for an answer as she started down steps, which looked to have been painted white thirty years ago. The door to the basement was old and dirty with a wobbly metal knob; a quick shove and it creaked open. The odor was dank and dim with two small windows covered with dirt and spider webs. We saw a light switch strapped to a supporting beam only a few feet away. Misty flicked the switch; six bare bulbs dangling from fuzzy covered electrical wires swaged along the plastered ceiling, lit up the entire basement. Cobwebs hung from every corner and crevice, with their collected dust casting ghoulish shadows. Four washing machines and one dryer sat at the far end of the area. Another door on the other side of the room had a sign on it reading, "Keep Out." We looked to see if the door we had entered had a sign on its back side. It did, EXIT.

"I think I saw a laundromat close by," Misty commented with a disdained look on her face.

"There's one up by the bus stop on Hennepin," I remarked. At this point, Debbie and I hadn't considered where we would be doing laundry. Nor had we considered that we would no longer have our petty cash fund from our change making business at Garfield Flats. We had used the laundry mat on Hennepin, back when we were doing a stake out. It looked like we may be making a return visit; for domestic purposes this time.

We followed Misty back upstairs and stopped in the kitchen. With absolutely no small talk Misty wanted a yes or no on the rental. For fear of not getting another opportunity we both said yes and wrote checks for our share of the deposit.